WRITE BOOKS FOR PROFIT

*How to Quickly and Easily Write a Book,
Publish it Yourself, and Sell It
For Unbelievable Profits!*

BY CHARLES W. ROLFE

ISBN:

0615671225 (10 digit)

978-0615671222 (13 digit)

First Edition

Printed in the United States of America

Published by

Hard Copy Publishing
Richardson, Texas

www.writebooksforprofit.com

Dedication

This book is dedicated to my dear friend Mrs. Angela Tenery. I would never have followed my dreams if not for her. She is loyal, honest, inspirational, fun to be around... yet she's serious, and often stern in her own sweet way. She could tell you that you had bad breath and make you feel good about it. I'm so lucky!

A special thanks to Angela's husband Trey Tenery... a most talented musician and gifted gun guru and to her son Marc Joseph Tenery... my assistant and side kick and buddy.

To My children

Lori, Scott, Vennesca, Alex, and Sam

You are my life! I love you all so very much. I can't think of a greater gift that a man could ask for than a team of lovely children like you. Each special in your own way, you are on my mind every day and every waking moment. Thank you for your kindness, your unbelievable tolerance and for your continuing love and support.

Table of Contents

Introduction

ARE YOU READY FOR A LIFE CHANGING EVENT?

Everyone wants to be an author. You wouldn't believe the number of people who've told me about the book that they're going to write "one of these days." The truth of the matter is, though, that it's not that easy. Just getting started can be a difficult process; there are so many decisions to make up front that it can boggle the mind and deter even the most hopeful writer. Once the process starts, any number of roadblocks can lie ahead. For example, many people are turned off at the first sign of writer's block – that moment when they sit down at the computer and *nothing* comes out. They try to force it or fake it, and when they finally do get words on paper, what is written is simply not that good... and another potential author throws in the towel.

It doesn't have to be that way, though; there are methods of dealing with any problem that you might encounter. Before I get to the good news that I have for you, however, I want to take a moment and make you aware of some of the obstacles that could lie ahead.

A book is a life-changing event, and starting down that road is something that is not for the feint of heart. The sheer magnitude of such a project can be staggering. A normal, average book that you can pick up from the shelves of Barnes and Noble is about 65,000 words. That alone is enough to scare away most people – it seems like an impossible feat.

There is also the commitment factor; if you write only a hundred words a day, then that is more than a year and a half of writing every single day without a break. Want to take weekends off? Then it stretches out over two years. And keep in mind, that's just the rough draft; there's still a long way to go. I've met authors who do a thousand words a day without batting an eye or breaking a sweat, and others who struggle over every sentence and can only produce fifty. You know what you are personally capable of, so do the math – it's possible, if not probable, that you could be in for a major time commitment. If you have a full-time job and a family, then you are not going to be able to write for six hours a day. Every minute that you use for writing must come from somewhere in your current schedule, so you have to take a careful look at what you are willing to give up.

Speaking of the effects that your writing project will have on your daily life, even when you've allocated those precious minutes of creativity, there will be things that come up to torpedo your efforts. They happen to the best of us. For example, are you going to write during your lunch hour? How about when a project comes along at work that demands all that extra time and more? Planning on skipping the gym to get in a little writing time? What happens at your next doctor's appointment when you've gained twenty pounds because you stopped working out? But those type of things are just the tip of the iceberg; you still have to think about all the other components of your life: family, friends, job, your kids' activities, work around the house, sports that you like, reading, watching movies, neighborhood barbecues… well, you get the idea. No matter what amount of time you set aside for writing, real life can come creeping in at any moment, stealing those hours from you.

If you can persevere and get your book written, then that is only the beginning of the efforts that you're going to have to put forth. You now have to publish the book, do promotion, market it, and spend hours looking for every possible way to get it into the hands of the public. Believe me, I know a lot of authors who get book in hand, take a deep breath, and then sit back to rest upon their laurels. Two things happen next: they don't make a penny on their book, and they never get a book published again. It is a total dead-end for that person as a writer.

Don't give up yet, though; read on, for there is hope!

As bad as all this sounds – and I know that I've painted a gloomy picture – I do have some good news for you. The book that you are now holding in your hands can guide you through all of these pitfalls that lie waiting for you. I've fallen prey to every single one of them myself, and I don't want you to have to do the same. I can help you plan your writing time, deal with writer's block and other struggles that you'll encounter, and help you find a way to realize your dream – to get an actual book in your hands. From there, I can help you market it, promote it, and make it available to the public. I have done all that myself, so I can definitely help you to do all those things… but it is still going to require a major commitment on your part. It is going to change your life on a day-to-day basis. You must ask yourself whether or not you're ready to proceed down that road.

If you are not absolutely certain and one hundred percent committed, then I would encourage you to step back and consider the project a little more closely. Take some time and consider what you are going to have to do… it won't be a small feat. Examine whether or not you want to commit to the time, frustrations and problems that you are sure to encounter.

On the other hand, if you are still ready to begin walking down this path, I can tell you that the end result can be incredibly satisfying. You can join the ranks of a very small community, at least in the grand scheme of things: those who have actually conceived, written, completed and published a book. If you follow my advice on choosing a topic to write about, which we'll get to a bit later, then your achievement can also be financially rewarding. It is something that I would not recommend to just anyone, but for those who are willing to stay the course, writing and publishing a book is truly a life-changing event.

There's an old Chinese proverb by Lao Tzu that says, "The journey of a thousand miles begins with one step," and that is what this book is all about. I'm going to help you take that first step, then the next, and another, until your journey is finally complete, and you are holding a book that *you wrote* in your hands.

Do You Drink Coffee And Not Taste It?

Okay, it's time for me to be honest, time to break down the barriers and bare my innermost soul to you.

Hi, my name is Chuck… and I am a coffee-holic.

Yes, I am a true coffee fanatic. There's no other way to describe it. You won't find me shopping on the coffee aisle at the local grocer store, though. Instead, you might find me ordering Mocha Sanani beans from the country of Yemen, Yirgacheffe beans from Ethiopia, or Kona from Hawaii. If I'm feeling nostalgic for a taste of the Crescent City, I might even break out the chicory coffee that I get direct from Café du'Monde down in New Orleans. My coffee pantry is literally a trip across the country and around the world, and I would humbly submit that it is unrivaled by any other collection that you're likely to find.

But I'm also a stickler about the way that my coffee is prepared – it is extremely important to me. You see, at the moment that I'm ready for my morning cup, I personally grind the beans to just the perfect consistency and texture. After that, I prepare the coffee in my French Press, in a process that can only be described as ritualistic. Finally, I add half-and-half cream to complete the perfect cup of java, and I sit down in my favorite chair… but you won't believe what I'm going to say next. Brace yourself, because I'm not kidding.

With all that selection and preparation, with all the cost and labor involved in the process, I really don't taste the coffee at all as I'm drinking it. Instead, I find myself getting lost in the daily news from the television or the newspaper. I start planning my day, thinking of what all I need to accomplish, and mentally preparing a schedule to map out every hour. Somewhere along the line, I just stopped enjoying the coffee that I go to so much trouble to prepare.

Does that sound insane? Well, you certainly wouldn't be the first person to point that fact out to me. Still, it is simply the everyday routine that I've slipped into – the act of enjoying coffee is in the up-front preparation, not the execution when I am actually drinking it.

That is a true story, but I'm sharing it with you for a reason: I don't want your book-writing experience to turn out like that. I can't tell you how many authors have told me that they fall into the same rut – planning the books is exciting, thinking about how to market it is challenging, and the preparation is truly a joy.

When it comes down to the task of actually writing the book, however, many authors simply go into a mechanical mode. I've had many people tell me, "I'm so intimidated by the thought of putting words on paper that I just sit down and try to plow through it." Every time that I hear something like that, I know exactly how the book is going to turn out. I read a lot, you see – and those words are probably a gross understatement. The delivery truck stops in my driveway every day to drop off a new book that I've ordered online, and I read each one cover to cover. My living room has bookshelves lining the walls, floor to ceiling. With all that reading, I have found that it is easy to tell when someone actually enjoyed writing the book. In some of the books that I read it is clear that the author didn't have a good time writing – just like I really don't take the time to enjoy the cup of coffee that I make every morning.

Ask me about the cup that I made this morning and I will be able to tell you everything mechanical about it: the region of the planet where the beans were grown, the texture to which I ground them, and the exact process of the French Press. I probably wouldn't be able to describe the taste, the pleasure, or the sensation of drinking the coffee.

It is extremely important that you put your passion for the subject into the works of your book. Don't give it a mindless, technical, rote effort – if you do, it will be evident in the final product.

I know that writing a book can be intimidating, but that is precisely why you've invited me into the process. I'm going to show you how to make the procedure not only painless, but actually enjoyable. Writing a book has to be a Zen-like process for it to succeed, and we're going to explore that together. Who knows, by the time that we are done, I might even be inspired to start enjoying my cup of coffee every morning!

It's In Your Head

I just mentioned Zen, so let's expound on that a bit. First of all, I'm assuming that you are actually in love with the topic for your book – if not, you should be. Once the book is completed and you start marketing it, you will be considered an expert on the topic. In preparation for that – and for writing the book itself – you should have facts, papers, opinions, thoughts, counter-thoughts, and arguments on the subject. Know the ins and outs, and the rhetoric of all the proponents, opponents, attractors and detractors. More than that, though, you should have a genuine passion about your topic.

I met an author friend of mine for lunch at a local sandwich shop, and the topic of books came up. In conversation, he told me that he had been pitched a ghost-writing project for a university professor. The pay was enticing, but my friend declined the job. When I asked him why, he said, "As much as I could use the money, the topic of the professor's book was the migration of the Monarch butterfly. Know what? I could care less about the migration of butterflies, Monarch or otherwise!" He laughed, but then got a little more serious. "I knew that if I'd taken the job, I would dread sitting at my desk every day to do the research and writing, and I'm afraid that it would be reflected in the book. That wouldn't serve the professor or me, so I turned it down."

I understood exactly what he was saying; you have to come to your place of writing with a certain reverence and respect for the project that you are working on, otherwise the book will suffer greatly.

There is a long way to go and many things to talk about before you sit down and start writing your book, but I want to plant this seed in your thoughts up front. The process really is in your head – you have to find out what is comfortable and creative for you. You need to start considering the perfect writing world for you, and the elements that will make it most conducive for productivity. For some folks, that is early in the morning, and for others it is late at night when everyone else in the house has gone to bed.

Think about the environment that helps you concentrate and makes your creative juices flow. Is it in total silence, or with some type of background noise? There is no correct answer; it is literally different for every writer that I know. I have one friend who puts the television on the Weather Channel when she writes because it is mindless and repetitive, and another friend who bought a noise machine from an electronics store that produces the sound of ocean waves to provide a soothing background sound. Still another has to write in total silence, and I actually know a fellow who listens to Frank Sinatra when he is deep in the throws of writing a book.

You may need to light a scented candle or burn incense to set the relaxing mood for your writing – many people do. Some writers say a prayer or meditate to put themselves in the right state for working on their project. I have writer friends that turn off all the lights and work by the glow of their computer screen, and another that turns on every light in the house to make it look like a bright, sunlit day. I am here to make a very simple point: no matter what it takes for you to write, do it!

A large part of the process of writing is in your head, so get your head in the process of creating your book, and minimize distractions, no matter what it takes to make that possible. I've given you several examples, but there are many others. No matter what you need to do to set your writing mood, if you are successful in doing so, you will enjoy and love what you are doing. Write with joy… relax and have fun. It will be extremely evident in the outcome of your book, and your readers will appreciate it.

THE ACCOMPLISHMENT FEEDBACK FACTOR

Are you still hanging in there with me? Good; I'm glad that you are. I started out this book by painting a realistic – however dismal – picture of the process of writing a book. I don't apologize for stating the hard, cold facts, because the simple truth is that most people who start out to write a book never, ever finish it. It's like that old cliché says, if I had a dollar for every person who told me that they were writing a book…

That's why I'm here, though; to help you through the tough parts, and be with you until the end, when you are actually holding your own book in your hands.

So far, we've pretty much been talking only about the challenges of writing a book. For the rest of this section, I want to spend some time talking about the rewards, and they are plentiful. I can honestly say that you will never experience a joy quite like that of being an author and holding a book in your hand with your name on the cover.

You'll be proud, and will hold you head high. Anything and everything that you do in life after writing a book will be fueled by the power of the accomplished work of art that you produced. You can do it, you will do it, and once done, you'll be able to do it again and again.

There is something intangible about wearing the moniker of "author." People look at you differently, and treat you differently. I remember one particular evening after having a book released that drove this fact home. A friend of mine was going to a dinner party and asked me to tag along. I didn't think anything about it, and since I didn't have anything better to do that evening, I accepted the invitation. I knew that I wouldn't know anyone there, but I figured that it would be a quiet evening with at least a good meal and some casual conversation with people that I didn't know. What happened when we got to the party blew me away. My friend was introducing me around, and he always added, "…and he's an author."

Soon people that I didn't know were bringing their friends over and introducing me as, "…the author." In this modest suburban party I suddenly found myself to be a celebrity. It was a strange feeling – I'll tell you that for sure. I didn't know how to react. The top five questions that people kept asking me were:

1. Tell me about your book; was it hard to write?
2. Do you have book signings in stores?
3. Do you know [insert any famous author's name here]?
4. Where can I get your book?
5. What are you working on next?

I answered each question honesty. Yes, the book was hard to write, but it was a topic that I am passionate about so the all the labor was worth it. I do all sorts of book signings, but my favorite ones are places where I'm speaking to groups. No, I don't know Stephen King, but I wish that I did; I love his writing. The book should be available in book stores, and online, but if you want a signed copy I'll be happy to hook you up. Next, well, I always have a book that I'm writing, a book that I'm researching, and one that is just in the thought process… but I don't want to jinx the projects by talking about them.

Now, I'm the least prideful or conceited person that you're going to find, but I'm not ashamed to say that the party was an ego boost like I'd never experienced before. I didn't put on any airs or try to be important – but I did enjoy all the attention. I was honest in my answers: I don't know Stephen King, my book really should be available in stores, even though it wasn't in all that many at the time, and I was kicking around ideas for several new books.

The same basic experience has happened in several different situations, and I never cease to be amazed how much people revere someone just because they've written a book. It happens, though, so get used to it once your book is complete. I call the phenomenon the "Accomplishment Feedback Factor," because it is a never-ending stream of positive feedback for the accomplishment that you have achieved: writing and publishing your own book.

A Boost To Your Career

Another benefit that will come from being an author is to your profession. I don't think that there is anything in the world that boosts your career like that of a published book. Consider the following examples:

- You're an obstetrician in a large city where there are perhaps one hundred others doing the same job. You present your clients, however, with a book on pregnancy and what to expect during that time, and it has your name on the cover. Instantly you're not only a doctor, but a published author on the subject, and therefore even more of an expert. They'll show the book to their friends, the other couples in the child birthing classes, and basically everyone that they know. You've instantly gone from one doctor among many to an expert in the field.

- You are a automobile mechanic with your own shop, like many others in your town, but you have a book on display at the front counter that spells out the twenty best ways to make a car last longer. It costs $17.95, unless a customer is getting repairs done that total over $100, in which case it is a free "thank you" gift from your shop. The book has your name on front, along with your photo smiling from under the hood of a car, and is truly a valuable resource for anyone owning an automobile. In their eyes, you're an expert, and even one-time, stop-in customers will be converted to lifelong patrons of your business.

- One of your favorite interests is the legendary creature Bigfoot. You're not alone, since there are tens of thousands of people across the country who follow the pursuit of the legendary beast. You interview people in your region who have sighted the monster, research information from years past, and dig for any evidence that investigators might have: plaster casts of tracks, hair samples, photographs, and recordings. When your book is published, you've gone from Bigfoot enthusiast to cryptozoology expert. You are invited to speak at conferences, you are interviewed by the press, and a hobby has suddenly turned you into an authority on the subject.

I could give you a hundred other examples, but you get the idea. No matter what your reason is for wanting to write a book, one truth that you cannot control – whether you want it or not – is that you will be considered to be an expert on the subject of your book. The psychology of the general public is summed up by one simple equation:

$$author = expert$$

There's just no doubt in my mind that if I were to do the research on the topic of "Wild Orchids of the Kalahari," interviewed botanists on the subject, gathered photographs of those indigenous orchids, and then put a book together, I would be considered to be an "orchid expert." I could get speaking gigs at garden clubs, botany groups, and public libraries around the country. Even though I went into the project with no knowledge of orchids, because I had a book with my name on it, I would be considered an expert. That's just the way that human nature works.

AND FINALLY... A SERVICE TO HUMANITY

We've covered quite a few different reasons to write a book, but there is another one that may not have crossed your mind at all: you actually may be performing a service to humanity.

I know, I know, that sounds a little grandiose. But in the grand scheme of things, you probably hold information in your mind about your writing topic that no one else knows. You have your own spin to put on it, your own perspective, and a point of view that no one else could provide.

That still may not seem that cosmic or important, but consider the Native American tribes that lived on the continent long before Europeans crossed the ocean. In many tribes, they had not only a Chief and a Healer, but also a Storyteller. It was that person's job to keep the tales of the people, and to share them with the youth of the tribe to make sure that they were passed on to the next generation.

On special feasts and celebrations, all the people would come together and sit in rapt attention as the storyteller stood up, raised his or her arms, and began to share the stories of the tribe from the very beginning of time. There would be tales of incredible obstacles that had been overcome by their people, great wars that had been fought, and the creation of the tribe itself.

You may think that this is just a fanciful tale, but it truly the way that the tribes preserved their culture and information. Consider the warring African tribes that fought in ancient times. When a village was invaded by a rival nation, there was one person that was executed immediately. It wasn't the Chief, or the Healer, but instead it was the Storyteller. He or she was the keeper of all knowledge and history, and without that person, the village had no individual identity… they could be more easily assimilated into the attacking tribe.

Why am I sharing these history lessons with you? Simple… in our world, you are the storyteller. Whether you are spinning a fictional tale or recording a factual work, your words will be captured in the collection of literature of our age. Your thoughts, opinions, and words may only entertain the readers, but on the other hand, they might have an impact that you can't possibly imagine.

Will your book be a service to humanity? Only time will tell, but the potential is there, and if you don't write it, then your musings will never be a part of the collective consciousness of the world. If you do commit the words to paper, however, then the future is yours to explore. As odd as it may seem, a book is an incredible – and important – way to do something wonderful and improve the world.

Ugh! Naysayers, Antagonists, Purists, Perfectionists, and other Evil People!

MR. FRIENDLY NEIGHBOR

We spent the first section of this book talking about the two-edged sword of writing a book: how hard it can be, but also how rewarding it can be. In this section, let's cover some obstacles that you may encounter on your journey. Some are individuals, while others are personal hurdles that you have to overcome. Don't worry, though, because I'm ready to help you with anything that might present itself to block your path.

There are many people that you will stumble upon along the way, and the first one that I'd like to mention is someone I call "Mr. Friendly Neighbor." It can be a man or a woman, and is usually someone that you encounter in your everyday life. A co-worker, the guy who sells you a bagel every morning, or perhaps the person living next door – literally, your neighbor.

When he or she finds out that you are writing a book, "Mr. Friendly Neighbor" will immediately begin to give you counsel… and most often, words that you don't want – or need – to hear. The negative words are bad enough…

- "Are you sure that you want to write a book? I hear that it's impossible to get one published."
- "Unless you're a Stephen King or Tom Clancy, don't plan on making any money with your book. That cliché about a starving artist is real, my friend."
- "You don't have any experience in writing a book… what makes you think that you can actually pull this thing off? If I were you, I wouldn't even waste my time trying."

Those are the kind of statements, however, that you will recognize as negative and will hopefully dismiss immediately. Beware, though; "Mr. Friendly Neighbor" has some other opinions that you are likely to hear, and these can be much more devastating. They're not outright negative, but are instead a kind of backhanded advice…

- "I think that it's great that you're writing a book, but that subject is all wrong for you. Instead, you'd better switch to a subject that I've always been interested in: <insert any random topic here>."
- "It's great that you're working on a book, but I heard somewhere that successful writers throw away the first pass of every chapter that they right just to get rid of the bad stuff. That's what I would do if I were you."
- "Congratulations on trying to write a book. Take it slow, though – I've heard that most writers fail because they hurry thorough the process. You don't want to rush things. Take your time… it's not like you're in a race or anything."

You may be able to see from those examples that the danger lies not in the absolute roadblocks that "Mr. Friendly Neighbor" throws up, but instead, in the detours that he places before you. I want you to be decisive on your topic and stick with it, and then use the writing techniques that I'm going to share with you to make your book happen in a timely fashion – I want you to be successful with the book that you write!

As you go through this book, I'm going to teach you to focus on your subject, set a concrete plan on writing it, and then help you to make your dream come true. With all the naysayers that you will most certainly encounter, "Mr. Friendly Neighbor" is one of the most destructive, so be on guard. Stay true to your cause, and don't let this particular obstacle trip you up on your writing journey.

"LET ME BE THE DEVIL'S ADVOCATE"

I cringe when I hear those words… I feel like someone is getting ready to rip my heart out. This is a spin-off from "Mr. Friendly Neighbor," and is just the kind of thing that you might hear him say. You'll encounter others that issue advice to you starting with those exact same words, though.

Whenever someone starts to say, "Let me be the devil's advocate…" I immediately put up my defenses. I don't want to talk to the Devil or his advocate – I want to do my work without that kind of negative input. You shouldn't listen to anything like that, because it is discouraging; it will take the wind out of your sails, and it can destroy your spirit.

The term "Devil's Advocate" originally comes from the Latin term Advocatus Diaboli, and was the name for a Roman Catholic church official who had been appointed to argue a case against a proposed candidate for sainthood. It was that person's job to try to poke holes in the all the good things being said about the candidate – to offer up any and all negative arguments that he could come up with.

Keep in mind that by the time a person was considered for sainthood, they were far and above the average Joe – most people would consider the process to be a "done deal." The Devil's Advocate, however, had to dredge up anything that he could to try to stop the canonization. Since it was part of the checks and balances of the procedure, he would throw up roadblock after roadblock after roadblock.

The "Devil's Advocate" that you're likely to meet will do the exact same thing, whether he knows that he's doing it or not. Often, it comes from a position of jealousy that is purely intended to spoil the enjoyment that you're experience with your writing project. In other words, he's convinced himself long ago that he could never write a book, therefore you shouldn't be able to write one, either. You'll hear him say things such as, "Let me be the devil's advocate here – ..."

- "...wouldn't your time be better spent focusing on your real job instead of this pipe dream of writing a book?"
- "...are you certain that your family handle how much time you're going to take writing this book?"
- "...at any given moment in America, there are hundreds of thousands of people trying to write a book; why in the world do you think that yours is going to succeed?"

Trust me, you're going to hear those things and more. I'm giving you fair warning about people like the Devil's Advocate and Mr. Friendly Neighbor because I can almost guarantee that you will meet them on your journey of writing a book. I see them time, and time, and time again... and so do the writers that I work with. I'm a big believer in that old saying of "fore-warned is fore-armed," so be prepared for these subtle attacks – even though they seem to come in the form of friendly advice. Knowing this up front will allow you to prevail over these wicked forces.

INNER DEMONS

Let's take a moment to look inside you; inner demons can be the absolute worst things about writing a book. After all, most every author suffers from doubt, insecurity, and confidence problems. I seriously don't know of a single one who doesn't.

I'm the first to admit that it's tough not to let those things get in the way of writing a book... and not just any book, but a good one that is going to sell. Having a good mental attitude is not only important – it is crucial.

Scientists argue about how much of our brain that we as humans actually use; some say 10%, others say 70%, and others, well, it's all over the map. The fact of the matter is that our minds have the potential to control many things about us that we can't even imagine.

One case in point is from a friend of mine, who shared his uncle's story with me. Something was ailing the fellow many years ago, back in the days before MRIs and full-body scans were routine. Instead, the doctors went in for exploratory surgery. When they opened the uncle up, the found that his entire body cavity was cancer-ridden; it literally had taken over every organ. All the surgeons could do was to sew him back up, and deliver the bad news: he had only a few weeks to live. They told my friend's uncle to go home and get his affairs in order, and if there were any last-minute things that he wanted to do, to take care of them immediately. Well, the old fellow did just that… but one of the things that he wanted to do was to travel with his wife. That he did. For thirty-some-odd years he lived life to the fullest, and the doctors just shook their heads and said that it wasn't possible – yet there he was. My friend's uncle finally passed away from old age, having lived a full and wonderful life. He simply made up his mind that he was going to do so, and believed it enough that it actually came to pass.

Another example is that of the four-minute-mile. It was believed for many years that a man could never run a mile in under four minutes – the feat was simply impossible, and beyond human capability. In 1954, however, Roger Bannister of England ran the first recorded sub-four-minute mile, 3:59.4 in fact. Since then, almost three hundred runners around the world have broken the mark, although it was once thought to be impossible. It's a simple matter that once someone actually did it, other people's minds perceived it as not only possible, but achievable, and it happened for them.

The same thing can be said for your book. If you go into it listening to "Mr. Friendly Neighbor," someone trying to play "the Devil's Advocate," or even your own inner doubts and insecurities, then your mind can be bent into thinking that writing a book isn't possible for you… just like recovering from a disease or breaking the four-minute mile.

I want to help you work on your inner feelings, to find ways to boost them up, and create tools that will keep your spirit up and running. Don't give any space in your brain to the inner demons that may plague you as this writing journey unfolds. Instead, focus on the feat that you know that you will accomplish – holding your own book in your hand!

PROFESSIONAL SNOBS

Some of the worst detractors that you will encounter are the professionals… the published authors who don't like newcomers, and the snooty English professors who are masters of grammar but lack imagination and ideas. They scream and cry about the poor writing and publishing quality of self-publishers, but the work that they themselves produce – although technically perfect – lacks in imagination, interest, and results.

Consider this example: there was a time in my life when I used to own part of a marketing company for the dental industry. We sold a marketing program to cosmetic dentists based upon a full-page newspaper ad for the dental office and a follow-up book that we gave to interested parties.

The ad we used was extremely effective. In fact, with one placement of the ad and a good team handling the resulting calls, the dentist could 'seat' around 150 patients for an evaluation, and 'present' about $150,000 in treatment plans.

If the dentist had any sales talent at all, he or she could sell at least 80% of that figure. It was a win/win for everyone – my company made money selling the marketing program, the dentists that used this system made money on their professional skills, and their patients reaped the reward of a beautiful smile.

At one point, I had a new client dentist in San Jose, California. I had to customize the newspaper ad with his contact info, bio details, and any other peculiar things about his practice that were important. As I always did, I sent the ad to him for approval before we ran his campaign. This approval was only for his particular details... not the actual body sales copy or content.

I soon received the ad back from the dentist all red-penciled with nasty remarks about the grammar and punctuation. As it turned out, his wife had been an English major in College; she hated the ad and criticized it because she felt that she could do a better job writing it herself. Her problems included a 'dangling participle' in the third column, some 'tense' issues, and a few typos and grammar mistakes that she'd found. She refused to let her husband run the ad.

What did I do in response? Easy – I fired her husband as a client.

In the world of copy writing, most professionals write at about an eighth grade level, ignoring most common grammatical rules in favor of a strong message. There is a limited space for the words, and a gigantic message to convey, so some rules of grammar are intentionally ignored.

Any change in the ad copy could dramatically affect the pulling power of the ad... even kill it. Remember that this specific ad had been used a hundred times all over the country with amazing results, and it made a lot of money for the clients. The patients read the ad and were attracted to the message. They wanted their teeth fixed, they liked what they read, and they didn't hesitate to contact the our client, the dentist.

My message is simply this: Don't let the professional snobs stop you in your tracks! Ignore the fine points in grammar, spelling, syntax, and just get the story written. There will be a time and place later on for you to get these things handled. There will be professional wordsmiths to do what they do best.... edit and help you polish your text.

Jealousy

There's nothing in the world worse than jealousy to cause someone to pick on you. Some people will hate the idea that you are writing a book. Maybe they haven't, or can't; on the other hand, perhaps they have and simply don't want anyone else to have one. They don't want you to get ahead because in their own minds if you are successful, it will make them look bad... or inferior.

Jealousy is a very real obstacle that you will encounter, and sometimes it is hard to overcome. I distinctly remember one such occurrence that almost made me quit writing; it was at a writer's conference that I attended. The conference had different levels: you had to register as an unpublished author, a magazine/periodical author, or a nationally published book author. Everyone was required to present proof at the registration desk before receiving their badge – either you brought clips from magazines, your books, or just stood there empty-handed feeling pathetic. The conference got even worse inside. The people who'd been published by national houses were in small cliques looking down their noses at the rest of the room, while the unpublished authors congregated together feeling like the great unwashed of humanity. The badges were different colors to immediately identify your level – and I know, at this point it sounds so judgmental and ridiculous that I have to be making it all up, but I promise you that I can name the conference and you'd probably recognize it.

The break-out sessions were color-coded as well, so that an unpublished writer couldn't wander into one reserved for the national authors. Looking back, it was a terrible experience! There was a definite hierarchy of writers there: nationally published book authors, followed by those who had been regionally published, then small press and university press authors, then magazine/periodical writers, the unpublished, and at the bottom of the list, those who had – gasp – self-published.

I can't help but wonder how some giants in self-publishing would have been treated there. For example, Lee and Sue Fox who wrote and published *The Beanie Baby® Handbook* and sold over 2,000,000 copies. Or Ken Blanchard and Spencer Johnson who self-published *The One-Minute Manager* and sold 12,000,000 copies. Those folks, while wealthy and successful from their writing, wouldn't be welcome in the top-tier sessions at that particular writer's conference, because they had initially self-published their own work.

It's a sad but true fact – many authors get caught up in their own ideas of status and superiority… which all comes down to jealousy.

I don't worry about jealousy, and I don't want you to, either. You see, I really don't want to feel superior – give me the success and money any day, and let others play their status games.

EDUCATION

Do you need an education to write a book? Many people will tell you so; they'll say that you need a degree in English and literature, that you need to pay your dues by practicing for years, going to writer's conferences, spending time in writer's groups, etc.

Let me tell you one of my favorite stories that may help explain how I feel about this topic. It's about a little book called The Christmas Box by an author named Richard Paul Evans. I first ran across this story when it was a TV movie – little did I realize the inspiring story behind it. Mr. Evans came up with a Christmas story for his daughters about a family who befriends a widow whose infant daughter died. It reportedly took him only six weeks to write, and when he was through, he printed off twenty copies for his family and friends. He had no aspirations about national success or a best-selling book – he just wanted to share his little story with people that he loved.

He'd written such a wonderful story, though, that his friends began sharing the book with their friends, and as word spread, people in city where he lived were going to local bookstores to find it. When Evans heard about this, he decided that he might be onto something, and started sending it off to publishers… only to meet with disappointment after disappointment.

After many rejections, Mr. Evans decided to self-publish and sell the book directly to bookstores himself. He printed 3,000 copies, and began to distribute the books on his own.

To say that his operation snowballed would be an understatement. He kept reprinting, and had already sold 700,000 by the time that the major publishing houses took note. When they did, a bidding war broke out between several major publishing houses. Simon and Schuster won the hardcover rights, and the 32-year-old author won an advance of over $4 million for his book that started out as twenty copies cranked out from the printer plugged into his computer. Before long, The Christmas Box made the top of the Publishers Weekly bestseller list. It continues to sell to this day, and a conservative count is that it has sold over eight million copies.

Mr. Evans worked well outside of the "classic" publishing model, and didn't follow any of the necessary steps of "education" that many people claim are necessary to be an author. You don't need an education to write a book…but you do need knowledge….and a few skills, all of which I'm going to help you with as we progress down the path of writing your own book.

In this section we've looked at a lot of negative things: how genuinely hard that it can be to write a book, the internal and external obstacles that will be thrown into your path, and even some of the detractors that you're likely to encounter. Don't worry, though, because this is definitely something that we can achieve together… I just wanted you to know the rough parts to expect before getting into the process itself.

All that said, let's start focusing on the positive aspects of writing a book. Trust me, this is something that you are going to be able do to – I believe in you!

Section One – Create It

HAVEN'T WRITTEN A BOOK YET?

If you have always wanted to write a book but you still haven't done it, well, there is probably a reason. I'd guess that you are having a problem with one of two things: either passion, or fear. That may come as a shock to you – after all, you've probably been blaming it on things like writer's block, not having enough time, or some other on-the-surface excuse. If you'll indulge me for a moment, though, I think that you'll see that most problems boil down to one of the two things that I mentioned. In this section, we're going to take a look at both passion and fear, and how they relate to your writing.

Passion about your Topic

Writing a book takes passion… it's what fuels a project and keeps it going. If you're not passionate about your topic, then perhaps you should step back and take a look hard at what you are doing. Passion shines through in your writing – but so does the lack of passion, and it's not pretty when that happens… you lose readers, get returns on your books, prevent fan clubs from forming, and begin wearing dark glasses when in public. Okay, okay, maybe I'm getting a little carried away, but the bottom line is that without passion, your book can easily fail… the cards will be stacked against you.

I've seen quite a few people who just didn't have a passion for their project; here are a few that I've encountered over the years:

- I once talked to a lady that wanted to write a book about orchids, even though she had never raised one, didn't study them, and really didn't know anything about the feeding or growing of the flower. When I quizzed her about her motives, it turned out that she'd simply seen an orchid display in someone's home and thought that they were beautiful. Now, if she were to put in a few years of research and practice in the field of orchids, I would think that her project could be viable. Otherwise, though, her lack of knowledge on the subject would quickly frustrate her and probably torpedo the book… she wouldn't have a true passion for the subject. I'd be willing to bet that the book would never see the light of day.

- Even worse than the last case, I was contacted by a gentleman wanting to write a book about pet care. When I asked him whether he owned a dog or a cat, he told me, "Neither, I just heard on the news that animal lovers spend a ton of money on their pets, so I figure that I can really cash in with a book like this!" I just shook my head – do you think that there is even a remote possibility that he could have enough passion on the subject to finish the book? Of course not! He would simply waste his time and energy, and if he did somehow manage to produce a book, it would be terrible.

- Finally, I talked to yet another guy who wanted to do a biography about his father's life. I was questioning him about who the target audience might be, but he had no idea. He finally confessed that it was just something that his parents wanted him to do, and since they were getting up there in years, he just wanted to make them happy. As noble as his intentions were, he wouldn't have a passion about the book, and I had no doubt that the book would be a flop. The fellow would end up with case after case of them in his garage, gathering dust and going nowhere.

These are just a few of the examples of books without passion. Want to know a project that I'd see passion in? Think back to the example that I gave a while back – that of a mechanic who wants to write a book about auto maintenance for his customers. Not only is it a subject that he's well-acquainted with, but he would have a drive to see the book completed because it would not only establish him as an expert, but it could also improve business in his automotive repair shop. Of course he would have a passion for the book, and I'm sure that the results would show it. Too bad this is only an example, because that is a book that I'd actually buy.

If you're attempting a writing project, it is important – no, make that *crucial* – that you have a passion about it. As I said before, if you don't then you should drop back and take a look at why the passion is lacking. You may need to re-focus your direction, or consider a different topic altogether. Whatever the case, you must find your passion before you can proceed with your book.

Fear of Writing

As much as passion affects a book, fear can be even more of a motivating factor. Trust me, many, many people are held back by fear. It might be fear of the unknown, because you never know what will happen when you go down the road of writing a book. On the other hand, you might experience fear of acceptance: will anyone buy the book, like the book, or even read the book? Maybe there are issues of time and money, and where those commodities will come from, or you may be worrying about where you're going to find a publisher. Believe me, there are lots and lots of things to fear when it comes to writing a book.

Fear holds many good books back – it prevents good writers from advancing a viable project. Just remember what Franklin D. Roosevelt said on the subject: "The only thing we have to fear is fear itself." He was a very wise man, because his words are very true.

Mary Schmich's essay, "Advice, like youth, probably just wasted on the young," was published in the Chicago Tribune as a column on June 1, 1997. It was widely circulated on the internet as a MIT commencement speech given by Kurt Vonnegut, and soon became the stuff of lore and legend. One of the lines of Ms. Schmich's essay is priceless:

Do one thing every day that scares you...

Are you afraid to launch into your book, to finish it, or to have it printed and hold it in your hand? If so, follow Ms. Schmich's advice, and go ahead and do that thing that scares you so much.

Potential authors get so caught up in fear about their project that they never complete it. Don't fall into that trap… if you have any fears about writing a book, just put them aside and plunge straight into your project. The more progress that you make, the more that you'll see your fears fading away.

YOUR SELF-IMAGE AND SELF-CONFIDENCE

If you get nothing else from this book, I hope that it is a feeling of self-confidence in your project. The great Maxwell Maltz captured this in his book *Psycho-Cybernetics: A New Way to Get More Living out of Life* which was first published in 1960. That book introduced Maltz's view that a person must have an accurate and positive view of one's self before setting goals, otherwise he or she will get stuck in a continuing pattern of limiting beliefs. His ideas focus on visualizing one's goals. He believed that self-image is the cornerstone of all the changes that take place in a person. If one's self-image is unhealthy, or faulty, all of his or her efforts will end in failure.

This is best illustrated by circumstances that Maxwell Maltz observed in his own life. Dr. Maltz was a cosmetic surgeon who operated on well over 25,000 people during his career. He did many, many surgical procedures to help his patients, yet some of the people that he operated on didn't notice a difference in their appearance – even though he had turned their disfigured faces into a thing of beauty.

The reason for this is that everyone carries a self-image of themselves in their mind, and that picture governs every single aspect of their life. It controls the course of the person's very existence. Job, relationships, career, everything is influenced by that self-image. Dr. Maltz found that if a patient had convinced himself that he was ugly, then nothing else that happened – even cosmetic surgery that corrected any problems – could change that image in his mind.

Maltz' greatest achievement came when he developed a process for helping his patients change their self-image… for healing the internal scars that they were carrying. He called his visualization technique "Theatre of the Mind," and those practicing it experienced a mental change that went far beyond any physical alterations that he made with his scalpel.

Dr. Maltz' "Theater of the Mind" technique involved summoning up mental pictures of the way one wanted to be. It offered the person the opportunity to "practice" new behavior and attitudes. This was based on the theory that the subconscious mind cannot tell the difference between an actual experience and one that is vividly imagined – a fact that has been proven time and time again in a laboratory. As a person begins to recognize their capabilities, he then imagines accomplishing the things that he wants to do, and then the subconscious mind begins to work out a way to make it happen.

One thing that Dr. Maltz incorporated into his "Theater of the Mind" was something that he referred to as the "step in, step out" technique – within your own mind, you replayed past events like a movie, and either "stepped into them" if they were positive experiences, or "stepped out of them" if they were negative.

Now, it would be impossible for me to cover all of the aspects and intricacies of Dr. Maltz' techniques in this book, nor would I ever attempt to try. I would encourage you to pick up a copy of his book *Psycho-Cybernetics: A New Way to Get More Living out of Life* and study it – you'll be amazed how much your life will change.

I do want to give you a working example of the "step in, step out" technique and how it applies to your writing, though.

If you are afraid that your book will be a failure, then you're probably imagining that your book will be published, and then no one will buy it. In your mind's eye you may see stacks of boxes containing your book in a corner of your garage, passing it every day and wondering why the book isn't selling. If that's the case, then you need to step out of that scenario. Imagine that you are sitting in a theater watching the scene like a movie; now, stand up and move to the back of the theater where the screen appears much smaller. You may still see yourself watching the same scene, but hopefully you're feeling more and more detached from it as an actual event.

Next, step out of the theater into the lobby – in your mind's eye, you can still remotely see the events on the screen, but they are no longer clear and cohesive, and they don't apply to you. If you practice this exercise with any negative thoughts concerning the writing of your book, then you will find yourself overcoming them.

Let's look at "stepping in," though. In your mind's eye, imagine peeking through the window of the theater door and seeing something new playing on the screen: half the boxes in your garage are empty – and you're opening others, getting ready to ship them to bookstores and vendors around the country.

Now walk into that theater, and look at the image live and large on the screen. Your books are selling, and your biggest worry is how to keep up with the orders! Finally, step into the scene. Watch yourself open a box of books, and count out twenty to ship to one store, and thirty to ship to another. Stack up another fifteen that must be signed and shipped to individuals who ordered them off of your website. Feel how real it is – and just take a moment to enjoy the experience… step into the scene.

It sounds so very easy, but to do it – and to actually believe it – can be a tough exercise. Keep practicing it and envisioning it. You can use Maltz' "Theater of the Mind" technique to picture yourself doing whatever it is that you want to do in life. The mental pictures that you invoke will become your reality, and changes will come into your life.

PICK YOUR SPOT

I have a writing spot, and I'll tell you right now, I love my spot! It is a source of both creativity and comfort for me, and it helps me crank out the pages when I'm working on a project.

You may remember earlier in the book I mentioned some things that help writers that I know get their head into the game when they're sitting down in front of the keyboard – listening to their favorite music, lighting scented candles, etc. The location that you choose as your "writing spot" is just as important as the atmosphere that you create. It doesn't have to be some secret writer's garret – in fact, it simply may be a desk in the corner of your bedroom. My only advice is that you keep the place special for your writing. If you sit in the same place to eat dinner, watch television, listen to the stereo, stare out the window, etc., then it won't be special... at least not for your writing. When I sit down in my writing spot, I know that I am there for one reason, and one reason only – to create!

When selecting your special writing place, be mindful of distractions. I have a friend who always wrote at the mall during his lunch hour, sitting at a table in the food court. It never made any sense to me – there were people dashing about, laughing and talking, giving what would seem to me to be a never-ending stream of distraction. I think that it must have been for him as well, because as far as I know, he never completed a single project while writing there. Now, I'm not here to pass judgment on your writing spot – what's distracting for me might be relaxing for you. One writer might crave the heavy metal thumping of an Iron Maiden song, while another might find the gentle strains of Mozart to be too much. Only you can judge what is best for you.

Surround yourself with positive items – I have several things in my writing spot that help me in my own writing, but more importantly, they make me *feel* like writing. When I sit down, I know exactly why I'm there, what I am doing and everything around me is focused on helping me do it. It's my favorite place... all writers have them, from the blockbuster giants to people working on their first book. Make your 'spot' special... make it comfortable... because as we go down this path of writing your book, you are going to be spending a lot of time there!

YOUR MENTAL SCREEN

Think back to the first part of this section when we talked about Dr. Maltz' "Theater of the Mind" technique. While we're examining the creative process behind writing a book, I want to introduce a variation of Dr. Maltz' method... I call it my "mental screen."

Remember the mental movie theater that we talked about before? This time, instead of using it to deal with negative experiences or enhance positive experiences, you can use it to experiment with your ideas – to take them for a trial run and just see how they play.

For example, when I was working on the last section about making your "writing spot," I was able to visualize my friend who wrote in the food court of the mall on my mental screen. When he was writing there, it was about ten years ago, and I stopped by to visit with him on many an occasion – and each time, I wondered how he was being productive in that environment. Still, on my mental screen I could see it as clearly as if it was yesterday, which helped me to easily write about it.

The mental screen is perfect for playing out scenarios that you're thinking about for your book, or rehearsing scenes before you write about them.

Visualization is a powerful tool, and I can't stress the importance of the mental screen enough. After all, if you can see your book expanding onto the screen, then your reader will be able to see it as well.

Developing your mental screen can take a bit of practice, but as you continue to project your mental images onto it, the process will become more and more natural. Soon you will be running your entire book on your mental screen as you progress through the writing process, and it will become a tool that is invaluable to you.

CREATIVITY... WHERE IT COMES FROM

Finally, let's take a look at the creativity process. Did you ever wonder why Stephen King sells everything that he writes – that guy could even sell his grocery list – but other struggling writers work for years to publish a single book?

That's a tough question to answer, because there are thousands of creative writers that don't achieve the success that some other authors do. Basically, though, it all comes down to the creativity process.

I recently heard a story about an ordinary person that was quite inspiring to me, and I want to take a moment to share it with you. A man named William Paul Young wrote a book called *The Shack* when he was fifty-three years old – just a year or so ago, in fact. There wasn't a traditional publisher in the business that would take it, but that wasn't Young's goal. It was a book that he wrote for his kids, so he had a few copies made and bound with a plastic spiral binding.

At the time that he wrote it, Young and his family were being evicted from there home, and he was working in a job that included scrubbing toilets at a small sales company in Oregon.

Word of mouth began to spread about the book, and so Young and a couple of friends started a company to print and distribute it. It eventually became Amazon.com's #1 seller in religious fiction, and hovered there for weeks. At the time of this writing, 400,000 copies have been sold, and another 750,000 are in the distribution channel. That little book called *The Shack* is still an incredible seller, and sales continue to snowball.

But where did Mr. Young's creativity come from? Well, to be honest, the cards were stacked against him. He wasn't an accomplished writer; the manuscript was never edited by a professional; the book was first published in a simple, spiral bound form; and he certainly wasn't ramping up to be a player in the publishing world.

Still, he had a lot of the things that I've talked about in this book so far. He had a passion for his subject, he had a plan – albeit a small one – for publishing it, he obviously had the self-confidence and drive to finish the work, and he saw the project through to completion… which is where it exploded into a success that could have never been predicted.

Obviously, not every book will enjoy the same success as *The Shack*. Looking back at his story, all the indicators would point to the book being nothing more than a photocopied, spiral-bound manuscript given to family and friends. You can never be guaranteed the kind of success that he's had, but one thing that we can do is to stack the deck in your favor, and give you a leg up on some of the obstacles that he had to overcome. If you have the passion, the self-confidence, and have overcome whatever fears might have been possessing you about writing a book, then the next section take all your creativity and join it into the physical process of writing a book. Take a deep breath, because it is now that time… the time to actually *write it!*

Section Two – Write It!

ANYONE CAN WRITE A BOOK

As you're starting out, there is one important thing to remember: anyone can write a book – anyone! Whether you're a farmer sitting at the kitchen table every evening with a legal pad and a #2 pencil, or a truck driver hurtling down the Interstate at 65 miles per hour dictating a book into a voice recognition system on a laptop in the front seat. Like I said earlier, you don't have to have a Doctorate in English or be a trained journalist to be a successful author.

You may also remember that I mentioned the Foxes and their *Beanie Baby*® *Handbook*; allow me to say a few more words about them, because these folks are my heroes. After Sue and Lee married in 1968, the couple used their entrepreneurial spirit to explore many different fields of opportunity, including art, coins, antiques, and writing collector guides. One book that they wrote and self-published, *Silver Dollar Fortune-Telling, a guide to collecting U.S. Silver Dollars*, was very successful. The couple sold it mainly through mail order, and it was the best-selling book on the topic for a decade – believe it or not, they sold over 120,000 books!

The couple was blessed with a child in 1991, and like most parents in that period, by the time their little girl was six the household had amassed quite a collection of Beanie Baby® dolls, a fact which didn't escape the entrepreneurial eye of the Foxes. They self-published *The Beanie Baby® Handbook*, taking advantage of the growing trend in collecting the cute little animals. To date, they've sold more than two million copies – stop and think about that... 2,000,000 copies of their self-published book – and have started an entire line of "unofficial" Beanie Baby® products. The book even broke into the top ten of the New York Times Bestseller List – something that is unheard of for a self-published book.

These people are truly inspirations, and are a perfect example of how ordinary people can write a successful book. In the years that followed, other similar books by different people showed up on the scene, but the Foxes were first in line as their two-million book mark testifies. If they had spent time worrying about the fact that they had no formal training in writing, or waited years for a traditional publisher to purchase their book and get it on their shelves, their success might have never happened.

What you really need is a good idea or topic, a burning desire to get it written, and the guts to stay with it to the end. Seriously, that's it. Everything else that you will need is available to you in various shapes or forms, but you must bring the basic tools – the idea, gusto, and toughness – to the project if you want to succeed.

You can do it… and, I'm here to help you.

WHY YOU MUST HAVE A WRITING SYSTEM

Years ago, I sat down at my typewriter to begin writing a book. It was only a matter of a few seconds before I realized that it was in trouble… I had no idea where to start or what to do. It appeared that it just wasn't going to work; I obviously wasn't meant to write a book.

Out of desperation, I just launched directly into writing an Introduction – after all, many books start out with an Intro. I typed for hours, and wrote page after page. At one point, it dawned on me that I was putting the entire book into that initial chapter. I was just writing as things popped into my head, and the information was unorganized and scattered. Everything that I wanted to say in the book had found its way onto those pages in one form or another… but it wasn't readable or coherent. At that point, I realized that some organized writing system was critical if I was going to write a book.

Abraham Lincoln once said, "If I had eight hours to cut down a tree, I'd spend seven hours sharpening my ax." Those words are particularly applicable to the process of authoring a book – you need to spend some preparation time before jumping into the writing itself, and doing so will make your job much easier than you might think.

To begin with, you must clarify the structure of your book by organizing your thoughts into an outline. From there, you can implement a system for progressively writing and completing the book. Just like Lincoln would sharpen his ax for seven of the eight hours that he had to chop down a tree, you should spend enough up-front prep time in your project. By organizing your book before you start the actual writing, you will create tools that will put you miles ahead of the average struggling writer.

I want to talk about three different of levels of outlines that can help you write your book:
- The Simple Outline
- The Detailed Outline
- The Masterful Outline, and the Socratic Writing System

The Simple Outline

The first one to discuss is the Simple Outline, and this is basically just creating a very minimal outline of your idea for the book. Stop and give it some thought; really examine the things that you want to say. When you have a clear picture of it in your mind, get out a sheet of paper and write down the main ideas in list form.

Let's expound on an example that I used before. Suppose you have an automobile repair shop, and you want to write a book on car maintenance. If you were to just sit down and start writing, your thoughts might drift from air in the tires to changing the oil to water in the radiator, all in no particular order or organization. The book would be much better if you started out by sitting down and making a list of major topics to be covered:
- Fluids under the hood
- Belts and hoses
- Tires
- Upholstery and carpet
- Regular inspection
- Taking care of small problems
- Car cleaning and washing
- Battery and electronics

After making your list, you can then go back through the items and arrange them into a logical order. For example, you may want to arrange them in the order of items requiring the most frequent attention: first "fluids," then "tires," "belts & hoses," etc., ending the list with "regular inspection," and finally "taking care of small problems." With your book organized like this, you can step back and easily see any holes in your material or items that you have accidentally left out. You're then ready to go to the next step… a better, more detailed outline.

The Detailed Outline

The Detailed Outline is constructed by taking the Simple Outline and expanding it into something even more useful. For every item that you have, all that you have to do is to create sub-points that provide a comprehensive explanation.

Let's re-visit the first item in our car maintenance example – the "fluids under the hood" item. It could be expanded like this:

1. Fluids under the hood
   a. Motor oil
   b. Engine coolant
   c. Transmission fluid
   d. Brake fluid
   e. Battery fluid
   f. Washer/wiper fluid

I'll bet that just by reading the expanded items above, you're already starting to see the chapter coming together in your head – even though it's not even your book! Just imagine how much a detailed outline will help you with your own subject matter.

I believe, and probably old Abe would too, that having a good outline is just the beginning. You will also need some tools and techniques for using the outline to improve and speed up your writing. Is there a way to take the outline and break it down into segments for writing ease? Is there a way to make each piece of writing almost automatic? Is there a way to make the words flow instead of having to sit and think and ponder and wonder? The answer to all these questions is a resounding, "YES!" – that said, this is the time to introduce you to my writing system: The Masterful Outline and The Socratic Writing System.

The Masterful Outline Socratic Writing System

Let's put aside the Simple and Detailed Outlines for now, and look at something that is more than just the construction of a list of items. I want to teach you a method that will not only allow you to build information layer upon information layer, but will give you the tools that I was talking about earlier… the items that you will put you far and above the average writer.

In order to get started and continue with the writing in a methodical way, I developed a writing system based upon my own experiences, information that I've picked up along the way, and suggestions that have been given to me by other writers over the years. This system is the one I use for all of my writing…no matter what I'm writing. I would implore you to give it a try, and just see if it doesn't make your writing life easier and more productive. Of course, nothing is set into concrete; you can add things to make it work better for you, take things out that aren't quite right for you, and basically make it your own. I'm now going to share my famous writing system with you, which I call the "Socratic Writing System."

My journey as a writer actually started back in 1985. I started developing a writing system designed specifically for writers like me – those of us who actually have to think about the writing process. And I have to say, even though I am constantly tweaking and improving it little by little, I have come to love this system. I find it extremely useful and easy to grasp, which is why I'm so excited to share it with you.

When I started developing the system, I wanted to find a way to create something that would be useful for anyone that wanted to write a book. After years of intense research, I think I was able to accomplish what I set out to do. Whether you have no writing experience at all, or you have a solid technical grasp on the English language, I think this system can be of great value to you. In short, this program will quickly and easily allow you to turn your simple outline into a completed book.

It's funny how and where we find inspiration in our lives. Who could have guessed that Triple-A – the American Automobile Association (AAA) – would be my muse? After using their unique trip planning system on one particular occasion, however, I was struck with this incredible idea to develop a writing system that could also take you from point A to point Z – and everywhere in between – on the road to developing a book outline. Not just any outline, mind you, but one that would be so detailed that the writing process just naturally flows into a finished book.

With the AAA trip-planning system, clients could simply call a toll-free number and provide the details of their trip... where they were leaving from, where they were going and any pertinent information about the route they wanted to take. AAA would then ask if you needed the easy and fastest interstate highway route, or if you preferred a more scenic route, which would be slower but more enjoyable.

Based upon this information, AAA would then develop a product called a *trip-tick*, which was basically a very simple and easy-to-use series of maps with written directions and highlighted routes. If you followed their directions you simply wouldn't get lost.

This trip-tick started right at your front doorstep. It would tell you for example, to go two blocks and turn left on Elm Street, then go three blocks and turn right on Grant Street, and then go 3.2 miles and turn right on Highway 90.... you get the picture. If you've used any of the online map services today, you've seen the exact kind of thing that I'm talking about.

These trip-ticks also contained small maps on the right-hand side of the page and written directions on the left-hand side. The point being, although it was relatively easy to follow the map, if you happened to get lost or confused, you could simply look at the written directions on the left-hand side of the page and easily get back on track. What a novel idea –

and this was long before online map-and-direction websites like Mapquest.com or Yahoo Maps became popular.

To make a long story short, I began realize that what I needed to do was to write a book. I knew that I could offer writers a step-by-step process that would not only keep them on track, but also guide them back when they journeyed off their path – just like the AAA trip-ticks. I realized how helpful this would be to writers who are struggling with the whole process. So that is exactly what I did, and you're holding it in your hands right now.

To successfully write a book, you will need to create an outline for it, or something I call a 'page-tick' in my system. You can then take this outline and expand it into something you can easily use to expand your ideas. Sound simple enough? Well, it is – so let's get started!

To begin using my page-tick technique, you will need to know what you are writing about. Begin by taking out a piece of paper and writing down the title of your book, followed by a short description of the subject matter. If you don't have a specific title in mind yet, just give the project any temporary name for the time being. For example, let's assume that you have some gardening knowledge and want to write a guide to building your own greenhouse. Your first page might look like this:

An Easy Guide To Building A Great Greenhouse

Everything that you need to know about the construction of a greenhouse, from where it should be located to the materials that you should use. Included will be several complete designs and their parts lists, along with step-by-step construction points. The book will also contain a comprehensive discussion of additional topics such as heating/cooling, lighting, watering systems, plant placement, flooring, etc.

The next step in this system is to list between 15-20 important things you want your book to convey to your readers. If there are more than 20 items, go ahead and list them all, but it's best to keep it around 20 or less just for simplification – you don't want to overwhelm yourself in the writing process. These are the items that will ultimately become the chapter headings for your book.

Once you have done this, go back and review what you have written. Most likely, you'll notice that some of the items can be consolidated into single points. For example, in the book about building a greenhouse, you might notice that two of your items are related. In going back over your list, if you see:
- The best directional positioning for a greenhouse
- The optimal elevation for a greenhouse

Both items relate to the location of a greenhouse, so they could be combined into a single topic:
- Location of the greenhouse

Try to merge your list items that belong together and reduce the overall list down to 15-20 maximum chapter headings.

Once you have your chapter headings in place, write these names on fresh sheets of paper – one heading per page. When you are finished, you will then have the pages to start your chapter outlines.

Next, make another list of around 15 to 20 things that would be important to discuss in each of these chapters. Just brainstorm – on each page, jot down a list of these things in no particular order. Think of these as sub-headings within each chapter.

Using the same greenhouse example, in your chapter on Location, you could list things like:
- Positioning relative to the sun and shade
- Availability of electricity
- Availability of water
- Protection from wild animals
- Protection from the public
- Etc., etc., etc.

This list, similar to the previous one, will again need to be refined into only the most important points. Once you consolidated these items, you should eventually be left with a list of 15-20 important points you want to include in the text of each chapter.

You'll need to make similar lists for each of the other chapters. Ultimately, you will have a very detailed outline of your entire book and for each chapter, you will have a complete list of things that you are going to write about.

But you're not going to stop there.

Go to the store and pick up a package of index cards. For each chapter page, take out enough cards to equal the number of items listed for that chapter. At the top right-hand corner of each card, write down one of the items you chose to write about in this chapter. Continue this for every item on the page. When you are finished, you should have about 15-20 index cards for each chapter. On each card, you will have one line indicating the item.

If we use our greenhouse example again, the index cards under the chapter related to Location of the Greenhouse should have each of the bullet items that were listed above.

Now for the secret... what I'd like you to do now is to turn the sentence at the top of each card into a question. In other words, change "Positioning relative to the sun and shade " to now read, "How does the proximity to the sun become important in the location of the greenhouse?" Can you see the difference? We have turned this sentence into a question, and that's very important, for reasons I will explain soon. First, though, take a look at the list of greenhouse location items once they've been changed:

- How does the positioning relative to the sun and shade become important in the location of the greenhouse?
- How is the availability of electricity a factor in placing the greenhouse?
- How is the availability of water important in the placement of the greenhouse?
- How can the greenhouse be protected from wild animals that could harm it?

- How will the greenhouse be protected from theft and mischief by the general public?

See how you've now developed discussion points out of your outline? That's going to be very important to the progress of your book.

I mentioned earlier that I call my method the "Socratic System of Writing." Socrates, as you may well know, was a very interesting ancient Greek philosopher. He introduced a unique teaching and learning technique called the Socratic Method, which used an engaging question technique for dialogue, learning, communication and teaching.

What Socrates accomplished through this Socratic Method was to essentially get to the point he was trying to make by asking specific questions of the people with which he was conversing. He organized his questions in such a way as to arrive at a plausible answer – it's a very interesting concept. What is also interesting is that centuries later, Socrates' method was incorporated into a famous sales system call the Socratic Method of Sales. Salespersons still regularly use this system to effectively close deals by asking specifically targeted questions that eventually bring a prospective buyer to a point where he or she will make a decision to purchase.

By using the Socratic Method, I developed the 'page-tick' that I mentioned earlier. The 'page-tick' basically outlines the index cards, and in our greenhouse example, you would by now have a written question on each of your index cards.

It's now time for the next step. Underneath these index card questions, you will insert two or three keywords that you think are related to your question. I call these "trigger words" because they will be used as a spring-board for your thoughts in writing each topic.

When you have finished that, you should have a stack of index cards. If you have 15 chapter headings for your book, and you have 20 points per chapter, you should have 300 index cards. On each of these index cards, you should have a written question. Again, under the question on each index card, you should also have two or three key words that are related to the card's question. While these cards are still in order, number them sequentially starting with "1."

The results of this 'page-tick' system will essentially produce your book outline. When you are ready to start writing, you can start with the first card and work your way all the way through the others in sequential order, or simply pick one out of the middle. Because your thoughts are organized sequentially, it really doesn't matter. In fact, in some cases, you may be better served writing some chapters before others simply because as your research progresses, new information will become available. But there is no specific order; this doesn't have to be linear writing – it is just writing. The 'page-tick' is there as a guide that can keep you on track, but make sure you number each index card so you can put your chapter and subheadings in the proper order when you put your writing together.

To use this system effectively you should take a card, read the question and then read the three keywords you want to write about in order to answer that question. When you start writing, make sure you use each of the three words in the first two paragraphs and then use them frequently while making your point. Work all the way through until you have completed that section.

If you sit down with the 300 cards, and you do one to three a day, you will very shortly have a completed manuscript. Congratulations! But before you break out the champagne, don't forget that while you now have a completed manuscript in hand, it is just that... a manuscript. It's still not polished, it's not proof read or edited. It is just a draft... albeit a completed draft.

But that's what you want!

Your job is to write a draft. You're not necessarily trying to finish the book or produce a polished piece at this point. Your goal here is to simply get your ideas down on paper. The polishing and editing will come later, and you can even hire an editor to pull everything together and clean things up.

That is the writing system in a nutshell.

Can you see the importance of the two main points in this system? The first point is to create an organized outline of your book. You do this by creating the 'page-tick' system of index cards filled with the questions and pertinent key points, which will ultimately become the body of your book.

The second key ingredient of this method is the Socratic Writing System itself. By using questions to elicit answers and by writing these answers down, you create your book. This process works because, as you have probably already experienced, it is much easier to answer a question than it is to sit down and just write.

Think about it. Wouldn't you agree that it is far easier to make your point when you are guided by specific questions? If someone asks you a question, it is much easier to explain your position than if you were simply told to write about a specific subject. When we are asked questions, for the most part, our answers flow naturally, especially when we are well-versed on a subject... which you should be if you intend to write a book about it.

Asking questions and using the Socratic Writing System provides you with direction. Like the 'trip-ticks' AAA uses, my 'page-tick' provides you with a road map to the end of your book. Imagine your road trip without any directions. You would likely end up lost, confused and overwhelmed. Writing a book is no different. You need a plan, direction and organization. In short, you need a writing system that you can follow every step of the way. You need the Socratic Writing System!

Using a Timer Effectively

Now that you know the basics of the Socratic Writing System, let me introduce you to one additional tool – the timer. Believe me, it's been a godsend in my writing; years ago I discovered how much a timer can benefit a writer. Actually, I think that I might have read it somewhere along the way, and just summoned that knowledge back up when

I needed it. By setting a timer when you're writing about each of the "Trigger Words"...say for 10 minutes – or 15 or 20, whatever works best for you – you'll begin writing and don't stop until you run out of things to say and/or the bell goes off.

Using a timer disciplines you, keeps you focused, and teaches you to write quickly. With this system it is extremely important to write quickly... to just pound the keys and get the words out of your head and onto the screen... or paper. The reason is that at this point you are writing a draft; you need to follow the outline and get the ideas and words down right away. You can go back after the bell rings and correct the spelling errors, and get rid of the junk that appears on the page, but during the writing period you shouldn't stop for that... just keep slamming the words down on the page.

Writing this way will leave you with what might seem like a sloppy mess of a rough draft, but I promise that you'll get a lot of writing done, and you'll do it fast. I also believe that your best words are the first ones...sitting around re-phrasing and struggling over each and every phrase will just make you frustrated and tired – and the writing won't improve that much.

CAN'T TYPE? OKAY, TRY THIS...

We've talked about the fact that anybody can write a book... but what if you can't type? What if you don't know how to use a computer? What if you are handicapped – you're blind, don't have hands, or have some other affliction that would keep you from typing?

The bottom line is that there are always options that are open to you. When I said earlier that anyone can write a book, I was serious – you don't need your eyes or your hands to write a book. With a little help you can use any number of other options that are open to you. Let's take a minute to cover some of them.

The Old Pen and Pad Technique

If you can't type, you can always grab a pencil and pad of paper and begin writing the old-fashioned way. Most of the classics of literature were done just like that. If you need to go this route, then it is easy enough to find a typist who can put your words into electronic format. On the other hand, there are many Optical Character Recognition (OCR) programs that can be used in combination with your scanner to import your words. No matter how you are going to accomplish the transfer into electronic format, if you're penning your book by hand, write the words as clearly as possible. Once your manuscript has been converted, you can revise and re-write. It's easy. Write on grocery bags or any kind of paper you can find…just write. We'll include instructions on how to find transcriptionists at the end of this book. Just promise me this – don't let the fact that you can't type slow you down a single moment.

Dictation and Transcription

You can use one of the same basic ideas from the previous chapter if you want to dictate your book into a tape recorder. One word of caution, though: if you're going to use this technique, set up your relationship with the person who'll be typing it into an electronic format before you start anything else. If you record your entire book onto tape, only to give it to a typist who discovers that your tape recorder garbled your words, you'll have to start from scratch. You need to line up the person that will be transcribing your book, and feed them tapes one chapter at a time. The people who do this kind of work are professionals, and many have special machines for running the tape with foot pedals to control the speed to make the work easy and efficient.

One added benefit about using this method is that it gives you a particular freedom – you can use a portable, hand-held recorder and dictate the book while you're in your car, at work, in the park, or wherever you decide to do so. In doing so, use your 'Page Ticks' from the writing system that I told you about in the last section... pull out a card, read the question, look at the trigger words, and then just go to town.

Voice Recognition Software

This may sound like something out of a Stanley Kubrick film, but I've actually used voice recognition software before and to be honest, I'm starting to like it a lot. In the beginning I hated it, because I always forgot the punctuation – you see, many such packages require that you verbally add punctuation. When I'd forget to do that, my pages would require as much time to correct as it would to just write them. After a little practice, though, I've learned to use the punctuation as I dictate and I get fairly clean pages that require only light editing.

Several years ago voice recognition packages were expensive and hard to use, making them prohibitive for most people. In today's world they are much more affordable and user-friendly, however.

The way that many of them work is that you will spend some up-front time "teaching" the software to learn your voice patterns. To do that, you will read one or more passages of written word that come with the system into the system microphone. By doing this, you are tuning the system into your voice and patterns of speech. This takes a little time and practice, but the time is well spent – before long, you and the Voice Recognition (VR) System will be working together as a team.

There are some pros and cons associated with this method, so lets take a look at some of them:

Pros:
- Since you probably talk faster than you type, your words appear on the screen much faster.
- The VR software spells every word that it recognizes correctly.
- VR software is developing rapidly – both Windows and Mac computers have voice recognition programs available.
- Such a package can be invaluable for anyone who is handicapped, dyslexic, or simply doesn't type well.

Cons:
- Although statistics vary for different software packages, VR systems can misspell anywhere from 5% to 20% of

the words. It also doesn't work well with homophones – words that have the same pronunciation, but aren't necessarily spelled the same – "to," "two," and "too" for example.

- You may be required to say word-processing commands such as 'New line', 'open brackets', 'Open file', 'Page down', which can interrupt your flow.
- Most systems require a fast processor chip and a large amount of memory for buffering and processing, and if you choose to save your spoken word as a file, it can take up a lot of disk space.
- The systems can be difficult to use in some settings such as airports, malls, and outdoor locations, due to background noise interference.

One thing is certain – we're all getting very comfortable with the idea of computers doing Voice Recognition. Think back to Kubrick's movie "2001: A Space Odyssey;" back in 1968 when it was released, it was quite unusual to hear Dave the astronaut telling the computer, "Open the pod bay doors please, HAL." Forty years and many Star Trek episodes later, we've become accustomed to humans talking to computers that recognize exactly what they're saying. VR Software in our world today is simply a giant step into that science fiction scenario.

Now, I admit that there is a learning curve involved with software such as this, but for a trucker or farmer driving a tractor, or a salesman driving between customers, you could easily write a book a week using this technology… if you happened to have a good writing system, that is!

Ghostwriters

Yet another way to write a book is to employ the services of a ghostwriter – a professional author who will take your outline and ideas and turn it into a book that you will publish under your name. You create a detailed outline as we previously discussed, and instead of making the "page tics," you simply write descriptive paragraphs that explain your ideas for each part. The ghostwriter will take your outline and write a book that is in line with your ideas.

This isn't a new concept – celebrities, politicians, and businessmen have hired ghostwriters to pen autobiographies, memoirs, magazine articles, or other material to be published under their names. It goes far, far back in time, however. I know a religious scholar who created quite a stir back when he was in seminary by proposing that several books of the Bible might have been ghostwritten.

Keep in mind, though, that the book will be your idea – your creation – even though it will be expanded and written by a professional who can do it faster than you, while still maintaining the originality and integrity of your work.

One of the biggest hurdles is finding a ghostwriter that is compatible with your project. Because of the ease of using the Internet, everyone from wannabe writers to published authors can establish a web presence. It's hard to know who to trust, and how to find someone that is not only qualified but will be passionate about your subject. I'm going to provide you several recourses for finding ghostwriters at the end of this book, but first let's talk about a few ways to secure a good ghostwriter for your project.

1. Ask for a resume. Be careful, though; a long, detailed resume could easily be fiction, and a short resume consisting of a few bullet items might be masking a great writer. The ease of checking sources in today's world makes the task a little easier. Does the resume claim to have written ten books? If so, they should all be online at Amazon.com for you to peruse. If they're national titles, then the books might even be on your local bookstore's shelves. Has your ghostwriter done magazine or newspaper articles? Then they might be archived on the periodical's website. The worst that you'll have to do is ask for the writer to send you samples of his or her work – or "clips." As you read the sample works, make sure that you like the writing style and voice, because this person will be representing you… they will literally be putting their own words into your mouth.

2. Check their subject matter. You may be holding the resume of a greatly prolific writer, but if he has penned 257 articles on different aspects of the internal combustion engine, and your book is going to be about the finer points of raising orchids, then maybe you don't quite have a match. Some people might argue that a good writer can take on any topic, but why not stack the deck in your favor? Choose a ghostwriter that had writing in your field of interest before, and you'll be ahead of the game.

3. Define the boundaries from the very start. Agree on the price that the ghostwriter will be paid, and assign the credit and ownership of the work. For this, a contract is essential. Payment is always negotiable, but is based on

several things, not the least of which is the immediate income of the book. Back in 2001, the New York Times reported that the ghostwriter for Hillary Clinton's memoirs would be receiving about $500,000 of the book's $8 million advance – of course, that is the upper end of the spectrum. If you're writing a speculative book, you may still be able to find a successful mid-list author willing to write for $10-$15 per page. The most important thing is that no matter what the other considerations of the contract are, when everything is said and done you own the work completely – you can do with it what you will, put your own name on it as the author, and sell it however, whenever, or wherever that you want. When you're paying a ghostwriter, the resulting work is yours to do with as you please. I'll give you a sample ghostwriting contract in an appendix.

4. Like I said, I'll provide you with some sources for finding ghostwriters at the end of the book, but if you're keeping the above points in mind when enlisting someone, you can end up with a well-written book with very little effort of your own… and while the book is being written, you can focus on your marketing strategies.

IT'S ALL ABOUT VOICE… LIKE TALKING TO THE GUY IN THE AIRPORT BAR

Whether you are writing your own book, or having someone do it for you, the issue of voice is a critical thing. Take a quick read of these two openings to the book from the earlier example of the greenhouse. Here's the first one that your reader might see…

"When regarding the lowly greenhouse, one must first give consideration to the varied aspects of its nature. It goes without saying that interested individuals have their own opinions as to the characteristics, orientation and assembly of such a structure, but the learned person cannot help from turning to the revered words of experts in the field..."

Trust me, the average person reading that introduction would be *immediately* turned off, and would simply toss the book aside. On the other hand, you could say the same thing in language that is more plain, but that the reader can relate to. Read this alternative opening, and contrast it to the previous one:

"If you're thinking about building a greenhouse, there are many things to think about before you start pouring the foundation. You'll probably hear opinions from friends and family about how to build it, where to put it, and every other aspect of the project. The main thing to do, though, is research what the experts in the field have to say in the matter – let them be your guide..."

The two paragraphs say the exact same thing, but in extremely different ways. The "voice" of the first one is pompous and stuffy, while the second paragraph has a very down-home, talking-to-a-friend kind of feel to it. Your readers will always relate to the second example, so make sure that your book is written like that – as if you're talking directly to them.

It is crucial for you to write the book as if you're speaking to a friend... don't reach for the "high dollar" words when the "hay field" ones will do. When I'm giving talks to writers' groups about this very subject, I like to use an example that I call the "guy in the airport bar" scenario.

Stop for a moment and consider this situation: you're at the airport to catch a flight along with a hundred or so other people, and the boarding agent comes on the intercom and announces that it will be delayed for at least an hour. Everyone moans, and then slowly begins to disperse around the terminal; some go to the rows of chairs, others take a bathroom break, some shop at the magazine stand, but you, and a few dozen others, go to the airport bar.

You jump on an empty stool, just as a fellow climbs on the one next to you. After you order your drink of choice – a cola, coffee, or frosty beverage – a silence sweeps the room as everyone sits and contemplates their situation. The fellow on the stool next to you finally looks over and says, "Well, looks like we're stuck here for a while. What do you do for a living?"

If you go back and read the two example paragraphs above, the first one makes no sense at all in that situation, but the second one fits perfectly… and that's how your book should be written. It should be written as if you're talking to a friend – or a guy in the airport bar – and your reader will feel like a trusted confidant, not a random customer.

USE STORIES… LOTS OF STORIES

Along with a conversational style in your writing, it is extremely important to use stories to illustrate the points that you are making – people love them!

Think about the last time that you went to the bakery and picked out a birthday cake for someone. It was probably covered with little curly-cues and flowers made of icing, and had different colors of even more icing accenting it. I'd bet that you had the name of the birthday gal or guy written on the cake as well, and then adorned the whole thing with multi-color candles. But stop and think for a second – why did you do that? A simple sheet cake frosted with icing right out of the package would have tasted just as well; in a blindfold taste-test you probably could not tell it from the extravagant birthday cake... unless you happened to get a huge icing flower on the latter sample, that is.

The truth is that you wanted to enhance the flavor of the cake with a visual appeal. If the cake looked special, then that would make the person's birthday that much more memorable and special. And guess what – it's the same with writing a book. You can put down plain, straightforward facts, and the information will be just as valid as if you entertained and educated your reader by adding stories to make your point. Stories help to drive your point home, though, and keeps the reader interested and attached to your writing.

This isn't a new concept. From the very beginning of time, storytelling has been the means by which cultures have preserved and celebrated their memories, passed on their values and belief systems, instructed, and entertained. Long before the written word hit the scene, storytellers taught through the oral tradition. Remember the earlier chapter when I talked about the storyteller in ancient tribes? Not only was that the truth, but it was a story in and of itself that helped make my point in that chapter. In fact, if you look back you'll find that I've been using stories as we've gone along, even though you might not have realized it at the time. A few probably spring immediately to mind:

- My morning coffee preparation rituals
- The auto mechanic who wants to write a book
- The couple that wrote the Beanie-Baby® book
- The "guy at the airport bar" from the last chapter

Take that last one, for example. I could have easily said, "Write your book as if you're having a very casual conversation with someone," but it wouldn't have had the same impact. No, instead I gave you the familiar situation of your plane being delayed – and who hasn't that happened to – then added the airline agent announcing it on the intercom, people scattering in several directions, etc., etc., etc. I painted a picture in your mind that would make my point interesting and memorable.

Even the New Testament of the Bible is full of stories used in this manner – Jesus himself loved to give illustrations in the form of stories, or parables: the Good Samaritan, the Prodigal Son, the Wise and the Foolish Home Builders, well, you get the idea. He knew how valuable this teaching method was, and employed it throughout his ministry on Earth. There are examples after examples throughout history about the use of stories, so there must be something to the idea… and there is! If you make stories a part of your writing style, your readers will not only retain more of the information that you're imparting, but they'll enjoy the book more as well.

WRITER'S BLOCK…NOT ME!

Let me say one thing up front: I don't believe in Writer's Block… I don't think it even exists. I guess to be more specific, I should say that I do believe that something like it exists in other forms or by other names, but it isn't really a 'block.'

Don't get me wrong – I wholeheartedly admit that there are times when it can feel like some unknown force has been sent down from the heavens above with the sole purpose of preventing any flow of words from your brain to the page – okay, maybe I'm being a little dramatic – but I most certainly don't think that it's some magical 'brain freeze' or blockage of any type. So, what stops us from being the creative beings we are destined to be? Well, here are a few possibilities…

Page Fright

Once I attended a workshop with an audience of participants that came from every walk of life and country that you can imagine. As part of the exercise, in order for us to get to know each other we had to individually stand and give our name, place where we lived, and a short description of our background.

I don't know how you feel about speaking in front of groups, but for me, the thought of it was agonizingly painful – a little bit like the anticipation of walking on open flames in my bare feet. As the introductions worked from the front of the room toward me like a rolling tidal wave, I became increasingly agitated and nervous. I had initially positioned myself in the middle of the crowd, so my turn was slowly getting closer and I could feel the familiar pangs of anxiety as they churned my insides. Despite all common rationale, as each person finished their introduction these feelings continued to grow.

If you have ever been in such a situation, you will understand that the approach of my turn only further increased my anxiousness. In order to try and calm my fears, I began rehearsing what I would say… "Let's see, my name is easy, I certainly know where I'm from, so I'll just spit those out and then say a couple of words about my background. After that I'll inconspicuously slink down into my chair and hope that no one really noticed me…"

Needless to say, the closer it got to my turn, the more nervous I became. I'm really trying not to be redundant here, but believe me, this was a nightmare. My heart started pounding, my breathing became labored, and my ears began ringing like the bells of Saint Mary's – in fact, I'm getting a little uncomfortable just writing about it.

When my turn finally came, I stood up in an absolute panic and tried to speak. To be honest with you, it was a total disaster. I could barely say my name, let alone recall where I lived, and then it happened… my mind went suddenly and completely blank… I just sat down; so much for being inconspicuous.

The point that I'm trying to get across to you is that sitting in front of a blank page or computer screen can sometimes bring up these same emotions and fears that I experienced that day. You have done all the up-front preparation, you have your idea firmly in place, the note-taking is finished and now, it's time to put your magically inspiring words onto the paper. "But wait!" screams your brain. "Where do I start? What do I say? How do I structure it? How will I ever make my ideas come together? People are going to read these words – what if they laugh at me?" Wow... it can feel like the weight of the whole world is firmly placed on your shoulders and suddenly you are left to do battle with every fear you've ever had.

Trust me, I know exactly how that simple, unassuming blank page can make you sweat. It can get your heart pounding a hundred miles an hour and before you know it, your mind becomes a feeble pile of mush that suddenly forgets how to think – just like I was at the workshop that day.

Then, like clockwork, the distractions start. Maybe it's time for a cup of tea. Gosh, I think I need to check my e-mail. Did I make my bed this morning? Did I feed the dog? Oh, I need to call my brother...it's his birthday. Maybe a nice warm bath would get my mind relaxed and moving. How about a game of computer solitaire? It is truly amazing how you will start to find every reason to get away from the task at hand and even better yet, come up with the most logical reasons to justify it.

It actually is a bit like standing up and speaking in public. Logically, we know there is no real reason why we should feel tense or anxious, but nevertheless, there can be a genuine tension involved. But with that said, I am here to assure you that it's a needless tension that we bring upon ourselves... after all, it's just you and the page ...right? There's no audience watching your every move. There is no one to stare at you as spit and spatter for the right words... or not. It is only you sitting there at the computer, and page fright is nothing to be stress out about.

Pressure

The deadline is looming ahead on the horizon and your page is still completely blank. Now what? Do you feel the pressure beginning to rise? Can you feel yourself starting to sweat as each minute ticks by with a deafening thud? Are you starting to dwell on all of those nasty things that will happen if you don't get this writing finished on time? And then, like a nagging itch you just can't seem to reach, that little voice in the back of your head starts screaming at you. Your reputation is on the line… your payment won't be sent… you'll lose your job… the power company will cut off the electricity then you will really never finish. Wow – deadlines and the pressure that they cause can be pure hell on a writer. Believe me, I know it all too well.

But guess what? It doesn't have to be an agonizing process. Why let pressures of any kind cause you to get nervous and lose your focus? Why let your creativeness be squashed like a bug on the windshield? Seriously – how smart is it to allow yourself to single-handedly stop what should be a natural and easy flow of words and ideas onto the page? This is a very real problem with many writers, but one that you won't have to worry about – I'm going to help you easily deal with it.

Boredom

Writing can be hard and tedious work. Let's face it, when the ideas are at a standstill, so is most every other aspect of your job as a writer. A writer's life can also be a very lonely one.

We sit in our little workspaces, sheltered from the rest of the world, with only our ideas swirling around and around in our heads to comfort us. We sit sometimes for hours, trying to organize a mish-mash of thoughts and opinions onto a page with even a modicum of common sense… let alone brilliance.

At times, it can become increasingly difficult just to stay in our chair and continue working. It is reminiscent of a young child that is told to sit still and eat his vegetables while all of the other kids play happily in the room next door. Not fun – not at all!

Not surprisingly, when you get bored with your work it can quickly begin to feel like pure drudgery. Once you start to freeze up, you'll find yourself looking for any way to escape the monotony, and worst of all, you may not even realize it you're doing it.

You see, the subconscious is an extremely powerful thing. When it has detected this boredom in your conscious mind, it sends out a terrible signal: "Writer's block!" Suddenly you'll find yourself sitting slumped over in your chair like a lump on a log just contemplating the carpet, chewing the end of your favorite pencil into splinters, or simply staring at the obscure marks on your wallpaper while not a single word is coming out.

Sound familiar? Well, welcome to the world of a writer. You are now officially a member of the not so exclusive "find anything else to do but what I am supposed to do" club! And I am here to tell you that our membership is growing rapidly each day.

So, what's an aspiring and talented writer such as yourself supposed to do?

If you have page fright, are feeling the pressure of a deadline, or just find yourself lost in boredom because you can't think of what to right, try some of these sure-fire remedies when you're feeling blocked.

"Writer's Block" Remedies

If you have page fright, just blast those words out there! Don't be too careful or introspective, because you might block the flow – just start typing. Forget that your great Aunt Lucy or first-cousin removed from Ohio are going to read your book. Write about something goofy and disrespectful, anything to get you started. Do you remember when you were back in grade school and the teacher would give you an assignment with something to kick-start your writing? It was probably something like, "What I did on my summer vacation..."

Do the same thing here – give yourself a starting sentence and go with it, whether or not it is related to your book. How about, "What I did on my weekend in Las Vegas," – just remember, what happens in Vegas, stays in Vegas... or you can only hope.

The point is, the process of writing...even if it's junk...will get the ball rolling. Motion demystifies the situation and writing goofy stuff takes the stiffness out of the procedure and lets you begin. Remember, you will always be able to go back and edit this stuff out, or even throw it away if you want to. Who knows, these random writings may end up being your best work yet.

If your problem is pressure, then it's time to have some fun. Wouldn't it be easier if you didn't have to write anything at all? What if you were finished and just had to do some spell-checking or scanning for typos to turn the work done on time? Would that make your life easier? Sounds good to me, but first you're going to need the text that needs correcting... so here's what to do. Don't take your normal course of action and type while you look at the words appearing on the monitor. Just start typing away on your book idea fast; really, really fast, in fact. Don't read your words as you go, and in fact, you can even turn the monitor off. Type as quickly as you can. Don't stop for anything... go at it fast and furious, without thinking about what is right or wrong, what makes sense or what doesn't. This next thing is critical: don't make any corrections, and don't think about stopping until you get every last thought on that page... whatever that thought may be.

Now, turn the monitor back on and go back through what you've written. Remember the wonderful idea of just having to do some spell-checking or fixing typos? Well, you are now at that point – just go through what you've written and enjoy leisurely correcting the spelling errors. After that, work the paragraphs and the formatting... that's easy enough to do, right? Finally, do a quick read and find any parts that don't make sense. Just delete or correct them.

When you are finished, you should have a rough draft in front of you. Now, you can legitimately take that much needed coffee break and come back to do another read-through to see what revisions are necessary.

Before you know it, you'll be finished with that section. The block is gone, and your book is quickly coming together. Best of all, you will probably be raring to go at this point, full of fresh and exciting ideas. So much for writer's block!

Something else that we mentioned as a potential roadblock to your writing was boredom. It's a genuine problem, but here's what I do when I get bored. First, I play around with music…I put on a *Gypsy Kings* CD and turn the volume up loud… that will get your blood pumping. I'll even sing along sometimes if nobody is around to hear me – I certainly wouldn't want to frighten the neighbors, or any stray cats that happen to be wandering by in the alley.

Next, I push my desk chair away and sit on a plastic milk crate with a pillow on top of it for comfort. It's lower, and there is no back support, but I sit there for a while so that when I do get back in my cushy desk chair I'll really appreciate having it.

I also take breaks: a short walk, a few jumping jacks, or just running in place to wake me up. I don't sit anywhere though – I just stay on my feet and move around. I find that simply changing my environment and doing something physical will break me out of my spell of boredom and get me back on track.

Next on our list of problems to overcome is something that I like to call "Blank Screen syndrome." There's nothing that bugs me worse than a blank screen. Since I work on a computer, there is always a screen and a page with a blinking cursor waiting for me. If nothing is on the page, though, it can feel like the cursor is beckoning me with pure mockery, almost watching me squirm in my chair trying to find the words to write. It can be horribly agonizing… if I allow it, of course.

To get rid of the blank screen, especially if it's stopping me from moving forward for whatever reason, I use one of the techniques that I talked about before – I simply begin typing. I write anything just to get the flow started then I slowly move into the text I'm working on. Once I am on a roll, it's easy to go back edit the nonsensical stuff out. One of man's greatest inventions is the "backspace key," and of course, lest we forget the "select all" and "delete" functions.

Another one of the top distractions comes from something that might not be readily apparent to you: disorganization. It's like trying to drive from your house to Omaha, Nebraska without a roadmap – you just sit there wondering which direction to go. Well, our old friend Socrates from a previous section may just have the answer for you.

Now, you may be thinking, what the heck does an ancient teacher/philosopher have to do with writer's block? Well, the answer is simple. If you're having trouble with the direction to take a writing task, it's probably because you're not prepared or you don't have a good writing system that can keep you moving along faster than a bullet train in Japan.

Okay, once again, that may be a bit of an exaggeration – but the truth is, having a good outline will keep you on track. You'll always know where you are and what you're writing about. Even better, a good system will keep you organized and focused so you can get the job done more quickly and easily. In short, it makes the process efficient. Socrates was the master of this. His visions and methods are still used today in everything from sales to writing. Go back and read the Socratic Writing System if you need a refresher, but it can make all the difference when it comes to work flow… or stoppage, as the case may be.

A Few Notes About Habits And Quirks

Before wrapping up this section on the mystery of "Writer's Block," I wanted to mention some typical writer's habits and quirks that make it easier to start and continue writing.

The first one is something that I call "the Holy Spot," which is my name for each of our special places for writing. I have a great book, *The Writer's Desk* by Jill Krementz and published in 1996. It provides some incredible insight into how writers work, or more specifically, how the place or 'spot' that writers have for doing their writing contributes to their quality and ease of work.

This book is full of famous authors and how and where they work; writers like Stephen King, James Michener, Tennessee Williams, and other famous scribes. There are over one hundred of them, each with their own story to tell.

In every case, the writer describes his or her favorite place for working and the tools and conditions they like while working. This gives an amazing look into the private lives of authors and what makes them tick. Interestingly enough, I found that every one of these authors had a special 'spot' or place to do their work that was comfortable, and arranged specifically to their liking. It was their foundation.

You know the old adage: a place for everything and everything in its place. Well, when it comes to writers, this seems to be especially true... at least when it pertains to our workspace. Computer, typewriter or legal pad and pencil, whatever your modus operandi, find yourself a 'spot' that works for you. It is just what we need as writers... a place to feel comfortable, a 'writing' place where we don't do anything else but think and write.

Now let's take a moment to talk about "combing the carpet," or getting ready to do your work. This is going to sound crazy but bear with me... it'll make sense later on. I worked for two years with one of the most famous copywriters in the world, Gary Halbert. We lived in Miami Beach in two seafront apartments and met each morning to review our work, schedules, and so forth.

One day, I walked into Gary's apartment and found him on the floor, on his hands and knees, patiently combing the carpet with a pocket comb. I wish that I was kidding, but I couldn't make something like this up. I got a little worried because I was certain that he'd lost his marbles, but he sat up and patiently explained something to me that I'll never forget... it was about his 'getting ready ritual'. As it turns out, everyone has a pre-writing ritual of one type or another, and Gary's was grooming the carpet around his work area – hey, don't laugh, he cranked out some awesome work.

What he did, and I do today, and will always do, is make my bed first thing in the morning before I begin working. I clean up the kitchen mess after having coffee, and you remember the ritual surrounding that, then I pick up anything that is

just lying around. I basically 'spruce up' my living space…
those are the words Gary used back then.

It's a Zen thing… one of many… that make it easier for me
to do the job of writing. For some reason, the act of cleaning
up and preparing makes it easier to then sit down and do the
work. Maybe it is a metaphor of sorts for cleaning out my
mind and readying it to go to work. I don't know, but what
I *do* know is if I haven't made my bed, I can't write…same
with the kitchen sink and newspapers scattered around the
living room.

Stop and think about the times when your writing has just
flowed – what did you do to get started? Is there anything
that, if it isn't done, pre-occupies your mind while you're
trying to write? Take a hard look at your habits, and find
what little ritual works for you. Find something you can do
that will tell your mind "Now it's time to get to business".

Okay, are you ready for an ultimately crazy confession?
You're going to think that I am truly crazy – and you may
even want to call out the men in the white coats – but once
in a while, I'll take a can of *Dow Bathroom Cleaner*, the
one with the Scrubbing Bubbles, and do some cleaning. I
just love that stuff; I'll clean the faucets on my bathroom
vanities, or scrub the inside of the toilet bowl… I know, a
little more information than you needed, but I think you get
my point. Just the act of cleaning something and doing that
preparation gives me a fresh and eager mentality and makes
it much easier to sit down and begin writing. It is like I have
told myself, "Now, you're ready – you have permission to
write!"

Finally, I have to mention the orange and the magic screen. No, that isn't the title of some new Tolkienien fantasy epic; instead, it's one of my personal writing quirks that works quite well for me. Sometimes, when I get stuck on something and can't get the words to flow, I use my magic screen. I learned this technique years ago and have always played with it at times when I needed some creativity or special insight... or just a little help with bringing an idea into form.

I have a mental picture of a screen... mine is a large TV – you know the one, that gorgeous 62-inch plasma wonder – but you can make it anything you want. I pop what I'm thinking about or working on onto the screen and begin playing with it... turning it around and over, bouncing it off a wall, changing its size and shape.

With this magic screen, you can do all kinds of things like testing shapes and sizes, creating schemes or situations. You can introduce characters to your screen and have them do things. You can insert a car, truck, or boat and take a ride. It's your magic screen and you can do whatever you want with it.

If I find myself feeling twinges of that non-existent "writer's block," I begin to describe what I see on the screen and then slip into the text I'm working on. Often, I use an ordinary orange; I'll pop it onto the screen and begin to describe it: color, texture, stem or no stem, scent, even the tiny little dimples all over its surface. Yes, the imagination is a beautiful thing and I can actually smell the imaginary orange if I try hard enough.

The process of writing about an orange, even introducing it into the subject I'm working on, helps me get the flow started... and thanks to my handy-dandy backspace button, I can always take that orange and the verbiage about it out later.

Okay, that's enough about writer's block; hopefully by now you have a handle on it, and can master any such situation that you encounter. I guess what I have been trying to say for the last several pages is that feeling "blocked" is normal, and it can be caused by any number of reasons. Since you are normal, there are ways to effectively deal with this imposition – because that is really all it is. Being able to write and express your opinions or views for the whole world to see and remember is an exceptional gift. Don't let something as insignificant as fear stop you from doing what you want to do. Let the words flow and watch as they create an amazing thing – your book!

NAIL THOSE FEET TO THE FLOOR!

I was attending a writer's conference several years ago when the speaker at the session that I was attending walked around the room and handed every person there a button. They were different colors, shapes and sizes, but they were all just ordinary buttons. As she proceeded with the program, the speaker finally revealed the significance of the items that she'd handed out: she wanted each of us to tape the button to our computer monitor to remind us that the only real way to write a book was to keep your "butt-on" the chair.

That was a cute way to emphasize her point, but her sentiments hit the nail on the head. If you're going to write, then you must spend time in front of the computer.

I've never been to the Maui Writer's Conference, but I had a friend that attended one year and brought me back a set of tapes from the speakers there. One British writer gave a wonderful presentation on writing, and spoke about the time that he came to America to run the New York Marathon. He was plodding along, getting close to the last mile, when he said that he looked over and saw a fellow struggling beside him. He thought, 'well, here's one fellow that I'm doing better than.' As they ran along, he looked over at the guy and asked what he did for a living. The man, panting and heaving, said, "I'm a writer." The speaker said that at that point, he knew that he could wear the fellow down – it would be one person that he could at least beat in the race. He resolved to ask him every dumb question about writing that he'd gotten himself over the years. Armed with the first one, he looked over to his companion and said, "So if you're a writer, what is your secret for writing a book." The guy looked over and said only two words: "Butt glue – you have to keep your butt glued to the chair in front of your computer." Suddenly the speaker felt like he was running with a kindred spirit, and spent the rest of the race encouraging the man on. Once they crossed the finish line both were getting liquids from the attendants there, and the speaker looked over at his new friend and said, "I never did get your name." The man just smiled and said, "Stephen King." As it turns out, even the masters of publishing know that the key is to keep your rear end in your chair and simply *write*.

Don't get me wrong, sometimes it's extremely hard for me to stay in my chair. I try to write a few sentences, then suddenly I'm remembering that I need to check my email, water the plants, go to the bathroom, get the mail, call Mom… so many things pop up when I'm working. We each need to nail our feet to the floor – figuratively, of course – or at least learn to stay in the chair for extended periods when we have the flow going and the words pouring forth. The worst thing that you can do for your book is to get up and leave at a time when everything is flowing. It's tough to get started again when you leave and come back. If you want to write and complete your book, it is imperative that you develop good staying power in front of the computer – like the lady said at the writing conference that I attended, keep your "butt-on" the seat!

REMEMBER, THOUGH, IT'S ONLY A DRAFT!

In the last section, we talked quite a bit about how to get your words on paper. If you used one of the methods that I outlined, even though you can end up with a finished manuscript, you may have one that is a little rough around the edges. Don't worry, though... it's only a draft, and there are several steps left to polish it up. In this section we're going to talk about how to turn your rough draft into something that is ready for editing. What is the first step? Well, you have to give it a good clean up, so let's talk about just how to do that.

Spell Check, Proof Reading, and Editing

If you're using a good word processor, then this should be an easy process – you can simply page back through the manuscript on your computer, and correct any misspelled words or grammar problems that the software flags for you. In my version of Microsoft Word, for example, misspelled words are automatically underlined in red, and any grammar issues are underlined in green. No matter what type of computer, operating system, or word processor that you're using, it probably has some sort of spelling/grammar checking function, and you should take advantage of it. One word of caution, though – take these flagged items as strong suggestions, but not necessarily the gospel.

Awhile back I went to a book festival that was being held at one of those massive stock car racing tracks that are springing up around the country as the sport continues to grow. Since the track is busy with racing only a handful of times every year, the track owners are constantly looking for other ways that it can be used – on that occasion, they'd allowed a book festival to set up tents, tables, and vendors in one of the huge parking lots. That morning, I'd entered on the exact opposite side of the racetrack grounds from where the book festival was being held, so I had to drive about a mile as I circled the perimeter. I was driving through empty parking lots that on any race day would be packed with cars, and when I came to an occasional stop sign, out of habit I'd come to a complete stop. The person riding with me asked why in the world I was doing that, since there wasn't another car in sight. I just shrugged and drove through the rest of them, although I did slow down a little bit each time. The thing about those stop signs is that they are on private property owned by the racetrack – a local police officer can't give you a ticket for running them. Instead, they're simply strong suggestions. On race day when literally thousands of cars are driving through the parking lots looking for a space, the stop signs provide some semblance of order. On the day of the book festival, at a remote side of the grounds, they really weren't a requirement. That's exactly how you should look at the items flagged by your spell/grammar checker... as merely a strong suggestion. For example, I tend to use contractions when I write – it is just part of my conversational style of writing. My Microsoft Word grammar checker flags every single one by underlining it in green; when I right-click on it to get the suggested correction, it breaks out the contraction into its root words. While that may be technically correct, I enjoy being a little informal in my writing. By the same token, words that are spelled correctly but that the system doesn't know are flagged as misspelled. When I used the term "Kona Coffee" earlier in the book, the word Kona was given a red underline, even though it is spelled correctly – Microsoft Word doesn't know that word, however. Like I said before, go completely through the manuscript and examine every word that is marked as a problem, and you can decide on a case by case basis whether you should take action.

When that part is done, I have one more thing for you to do that is simply magic. I'm going to tell you one of the secrets of self-editing... are you ready? This is something huge, so prepare yourself... the secret to getting your manuscript ready for editing is quite simple:

Read your manuscript out loud.

Sounds simple, right? Well, there is something about reading your manuscript out loud that will help you in ways that you can't possibly imagine. When I do it, I hear every little problem – repeated words, pauses where they aren't needed (or where they are), run-on sentences, and all the other problems that plague every writer's manuscript.

I want to really encourage you to do this – you won't believe the number of things that you will find in the words that you've written.

When you've finished your spelling, grammar, and reading aloud passes, it is time to give your manuscript to someone else to read. Not a professional editor, mind you, but a friend who can give you some good, constructive comments on your book. I'm not talking about someone who fits the description of "Mr. Friendly Neighbor" or "The Devil's Advocate" that we discussed earlier – select a friend that won't mind giving the manuscript a fair read, and marking anything that they notice. It would be helpful if the person knew something about the English language, even if only comes from the fact that he or she loves to read and goes through a book or so every week. If your reader knows something about the subject matter, then all the better. When I do this, I print out the manuscript for them, double-spaced on regular letter-sized paper with one-inch margins. I'll also buy them a new red pen, and ask that they mark any and everything, even if they're not exactly sure about it. These include:

- Words that are possibly misspelled or used incorrectly
- Awkward or repeated wording
- Sentences that are way too long – these are known as "run-on" sentences
- Passages that seem out of place or that don't make sense
- …or ANYTHING that makes their flow of reading stop or even pause

When I get the manuscript back, then I'll do the same that I did with the results from my spell/grammar checker – I'll go through the pages, and consider everything that they marked on a case by case basis. I give a lot of stock to any comment that says something like, "I had to read this paragraph a couple of times to get it," or "The wording of this sentence tripped me up as I was reading along." We get so close to our own work that it's like our child; often we can't see the flaws even though they are staring us right in the face.

A couple of years ago I had just completed a particular book and had taken it up to the point where I needed a friend to read it. When he was done, we met for coffee to go over the things that he'd found. Many of the items that he had marked were exactly the kinds of flags that I expected... but then I came to one entire paragraph with huge red "X's" across each page. My friend must have noticed my puzzled expression, because he said, "Oh, you're at that chapter. Well, I hate to say it, but it makes no sense. I don't know why it's there, or why it's even in the book. You should consider taking that out completely." I immediately went on the defensive, stammering out what a great chapter it actually was, and how he simply didn't understand how it fit into the whole picture. He just sat there smiling, and finally pointed out, "You know, you sound exactly like a defense attorney trying to save his client's life in a murder trial." That image stopped me for a second, and I just sat there stunned – I hated to admit it, but that was *exactly* what I was doing. I had to laugh, and I told my friend I'd go back and give it another read. I think that he jolted me enough into reality that when I re-read the manuscript, I had to agree with his assessment. That chapter was useless, and was basically just me trying to be clever. As I've said before, thank goodness for the "delete" key.

After you have folded in your friend's comments, your manuscript is now ready for a professional editor. Warning: this is a step that many writers are tempted to skip. After all, you've read it through a time or two yourself, your friend has given it a good read, so it must be near perfect – right?

Wrong! Believe me, without the trained eye of a professional, your book will reek of 'amateurism'. They will be clinical and impartial when doing their editing pass, and can therefore make recommendations that both you and your friend will have missed. It is an extra expense, but one that will be well worth the investment in the log run. I'm including a guide to finding an editor in an appendix at the end of the book.

Research

While the book is on the editor's desk, you'll have a little extra time on your hands. In fact, you might find yourself pacing back and forth like an expectant parent waiting for a baby to be born. One thing that I always do to fill the time is to finish up any necessary research on the book. In fact, I usually leave any research for this time. If I'm on a roll while I'm writing the book and I need to know some statistic such as, for example, the percentage of people with above a high school education who live in a region of the U.S., I'll just put a marker there and keep writing. I'll do the same with other numbers, dates, or anything that needs looking up – it buys me time and doesn't interrupt my flow of writing. You can use whatever marker makes sense to you, but one that I like is "TBD" – short for "To Be Determined." In fact, if I were writing a book on household plumbing, a paragraph in my manuscript might look this:

It is extremely important to pressure-test all joints in a water line at full pressure. Although Schedule 40 PVC pipe is rated for use in most every plumbing situation, a study conducted in 2007(TBD) indicates that 1 out of every 5,000(TBD) pieces contain a manufacturing flaw that will cause a failure in the line.

If I was writing that book, I might know that there is a certain percentage of flaws in PVC pipe and joint manufacturing, but instead of stopping to look up the percentage right that moment I could simply flag it with a "TBD" and keep going.

When I give the manuscript to my editor, I simply tell him or her to ignore any "TBD" markings and pretend that they aren't there. As the script is being edited, I'll do a search for the term TBD and start researching each one individually. As I get the correct answers, I fill them in, and keep going with the next one. There are several ways to organize this:

- Print out a copy of the manuscript and write in the answer to each TBD in red ink so that you'll be able to locate them later.
- Keep a list with items such as, "Chapter 3, page 1, paragraph 2: TBD = 3 meters".
- Type them into a copy of the software version of the manuscript, leaving the "TBD" marks there so that you can search and find them later.

No matter how you manage your research, make sure that once you get your manuscript back from the editor you'll be able to replace all the TBD values with the ones that you verified in this post-writing research phase of your book.

The Revision Process

When the professional editor returns your manuscript, it will be marked up with grammatical corrections, editorial suggestions, and a myriad of other items for you to consider. At that point, it is time to sit down with your original manuscript, the edited version, and your "TBD" research. Your job will be to fold them all together into a single, completed manuscript.

There's one thing that I have to warn you about – this can be a juggling act! I can't tell you how many times I've been doing this very thing, carefully adding the edits to the final version of the manuscript, only to find out that for some unknown length of time I'd been actually editing the software copy of the "TBD" research version. It's frustrating, and the only way to be sure that everything is in is to start from scratch… a complete re-do.

While it is important to keep the individual files separate during the process, perhaps something that is even more important is to keep a backup of everything. Make sure that if you do need to drop back and re-start because of any problem, you can do so without missing a beat.

Now then, adding your "TBD" values will be easy, but you may encounter some marks made by the editor that are unfamiliar to you. The following table of common will help you understand exactly what the editor is trying to tell you with his or her abbreviations and notes:

Abbreviation	Meaning	Description
_℮_	Delete word(s)	This scribble is editor-speak meaning to delete the word(s) that this mark refers to – usually where the scribble starts.
#	Space Needed	Insert a space where this symbol marks.
∧	Insert	This mark, like a little teepee, will usually have a word or phrase under it (or above it, if the mark is inverted). Insert the new word or phrase at the point indicated.
¶	Paragraph	Sometimes written as a "c" with two vertical lines beside it, this means to begin a new paragraph at the indicated point.
abbr	abbreviation	The editor is objecting to your use of an abbreviation, such as 1st instead of first.
Awk	Awkward	Even though it may be technically correct, the wording indicated reads awkwardly and should be re-written.
caps	Capital letters	The word(s) that this appears beside should be capitalized.
Cliché	The phrase is a cliché	The marked text is a tired, overused cliché that should be replaced.
Contr	Contraction	Some editors mark all contractions such as don't, can't, or won't, as incorrect.
Dangles	Dangling Phrase	A dependent phrase isn't attached to anything, or is attached to something incorrectly. Example, "Walking down the street, a church bell chimed." You may mean that a person walking down a street heard a church bell chiming in the distance, but grammatically the sentences says that a church bell was walking down the street when it chimed.

Abbreviation	Meaning	Description
lc	Lower case	The word(s) that this appears beside should be lower case.
Not sentence	The words do not form a sentence	Even though it looks like a sentence, the marked text has no subject or no predicate, or it is framed as a clause that shouldn't stand alone.
Nsw	No such word	The word doesn't exist, or is not in the common knowledge base. Replace it.
purp	Purple prose	Getting more and more uncommon, this mark means that the text associated with it is over-the-top, and should be toned down a bit.
Refers to?	Pronoun reference is unclear	The editor is confused as to which noun the marked pronoun refers to. For example, in the passage: "I hit the ball, which disappeared over the right field fence. It was wonderful." The pronoun "it" doesn't refer to any of the nouns I, ball, or fence. Instead it refers to an implied noun "the feeling" – the editor is pointing out that something like this could be confusing to the reader.
Run on	A run-on sentence.	This is a really, really, really long sentence that reads awkwardly, or two or more complete sentences that are combined using commas or other punctuation to connect them making the whole awkwardly long; run-on sentences are very common, and should be avoided. (That explanation was a run-on sentence, by the way)

Abbreviation	Meaning	Description
Sp	Spelling	The flagged word is spelled incorrectly.
Stet	Let it stand	This is the editor saying, "oops – I marked something incorrectly… leave it as it is."
Wc	Word choice	A word or phrase is used incorrectly or in the wrong context – replace it.
Ww	Wrong word	A word or phrase actually means something different than what you think that it does.

Different editors may use their own, custom marks, new ones that may have come into vogue, or older ones that are outdated. If you have any question at all about what a particular instruction means, don't guess – go directly to the editor.

I almost always take an editor's word for something mechanical, like punctuation, or an indication that a passage was wordy or confusing. The thing that I'm careful about, though, is following his or her advice when in conflicts with my conversational writing style. Face it, I use contractions and partial sentences all the time. All the time! (oops, there was another one, AND it used an exclamation mark, something else that editors detest). I don't want my writing to be stuffy and formal, but I do want it to be grammatically correct, at least within the confines of my little world, and a professional editor is the one that makes that happen.

Pass It On

Okay, your manuscript is complete, all edits have been done, and you're ready to proceed. Before jumping into the world of publishing, though, it is time to pass the book around for opinions and comments. Once again, let me say that this isn't an invitation for interaction with "Mr. Friendly Neighbor" or "The Devil's Advocate" – instead, this is an exercise in gathering testimonials and praise. After all, the friend's read and your editor's pass have both helped you through rough spots, so you are now done with the editing process. You should now be turning your attention to printing and selling the book, and to do that you will need reviews and recommendations.

I usually contact friends of mine who have a published book, work in the publishing world, or are in my field of expertise. This is important to remember. Why? Well, suppose that you had the following quote on your book's back cover:

"A fantastic book… I couldn't put it down!"

– Michael Bishop

When someone picks up your book and sees that, the reader won't be contemplating the glowing review. Instead, he's going to be thinking, "Who in the heck is Michael Bishop, and why should I believe what he says?"

On the other hand, imagine the quote instead read something like this:

*"A fantastic book… I couldn't put it down!" – Michael Bishop, author of the new book, **One Month To A Better You!***

Now the reader will glance at the name, see that it is a published author, and can then turn his attention to the review blurb itself. That's just human nature – it doesn't matter whether the press kit reader has heard of the author or the book. There's something about being a published author that people automatically respect, just like I mentioned earlier in this book.

When I'm at this stage, I contact some of my friends with books and ask them to read a few sample, representative chapters, then give me a blurb if they felt comfortable in doing so. Since this request is only made of a few friends, they are usually anxious to help out. A side benefit for them in providing the quote is that their name and latest credit would be in front of every person who reads the back cover of the book. Name recognition is priceless in the publishing world, and every little bit helps. Within a couple of days from making my question, I usually have enough quotes to use in the book.

There's one more question that I always get on this item, though, and that is: "What if I don't know anyone who's written a book?" There is another solution to this problem, and chances are, you'll be able to do it quite easily.

Most authors write about something they know, or something that they're interested in. That means that the author probably knows several people involved it as well who could lend a blurb. For example, if you've written a cookbook, you could get reviews by people in the food business that you know: the chef of a local restaurant that you frequent, the manager of a gourmet grocery where you shop, or the owner of a specialty coffee boutique. Anyone whose title can lend credibility to your back cover will work well. It should be written as:

> *"A wonderful book... scrumptious recipes!"*
> – **Ronnie Jackson**, *gourmet chef and owner of Chez Paris*

Have fun with this – but keep your sources credible, and quote them accurately.

YOU'VE JUST WRITTEN A BOOK... NOW WHAT?!?

Congratulations... when you've reached this point, you have accomplished very few writers ever do – you've completed a book!

That's the hardest part of the project that was facing you. The rest of the process is just mechanical... although getting the book published is a daunting task to most people, I've been there before and I am going to make it easy for you. In the next section we're going to talk about all the ins and outs of publishing your book. Before we go there, though, take a moment to relax and celebrate for a moment. Maybe it's time to have a glass of wine out on the front porch of your house, or sip a cup of coffee back on the patio – maybe it's even time to take a deep breath, close out your files, and turn in for the evening, secure in the knowledge that you have conquered an extraordinary mountain.

When you're ready, turn the page for the next section, and we'll start down the road of actually getting your book published and into your hands.

Section Three – Publish It!

Okay, we've delved into the process of creating a book, and then talked about the mechanics of how to write it, so it is now time to examine the different avenues of publication that are open to you. As we start looking at them, keep in mind that there are no right or wrong solutions to getting your book published – you just need to find the one that best suits your needs, while being wary of the people who are just out to make a buck off of you.

WHAT'S OUT THERE?

There are hundreds, if not thousands of places to publish a book. They range from the old, traditional publishing houses, to vanity presses, to publishers employing the latest, new technology… it can be a confusing world. Don't worry, though, as we go through this section together you're soon going to be very comfortable with the all the different options – and I think that you'll see why some are bad, some are *really* bad, but others hold a lot of potential. Let's get started.

Traditional Publishing Houses

This is what every author dreams of when starting down the path of their writing career. Believe me, we've all had these thoughts and dreams, and they go something like this:

- You pen a brilliant manuscript
- After sending it off to a publisher, you receive a contract in short order

- The contract includes a healthy advance, and generous royalty schedule
- Within a few months, your book is in stores nationwide, and the money starts rolling in like a tsunami as you sit back and contemplate your next great work

I once held that exact scenario in my head as the one and only way that books were published. The problem with that idea is that the publishing world simply doesn't work like that – at least, not anymore. These days the major publishing houses are all owned by huge international companies, who don't care a bit about the state of American literature. Their only bottom line is profit, and they're taking fewer and fewer chances on new, unproven authors. Face it, they can statistically show what return they'll get on a John Grisham or Stephen King book, so it is difficult for them to justify pouring any money into a new face on the block.

Time is also an issue for you to consider; send a manuscript off to a major publishing house, and you may not hear back for six months. If you get a flush letter, then you have to re-group and start over with another publisher. After another six months, if you're flushed again you have to find another place to send it, and well, you can see the time investment.

Another consideration is that many large publishers accept only agented manuscripts, so you may have to first spend the time to acquire an agent – which can take as long as finding a publisher, if not longer – all before a major house ever sees your manuscript.

Now it's time for some tough love: if your book is picked up by a publisher, then you're going to be paid a small commission on books sold... and not much more. Believe me, it's time for a revolution in the publishing world, because the authors simply don't make that much money per book. Consider what Forbes Magazine said on the subject in May of 2008:

> *"Technology has disrupted every industry. Now, it's book publishing's turn. Archaic beyond belief, it's an industry that treats its most important asset – the author – badly. Can this go on? The book market in the United States is worth about $32 billion a year; the rest of the world, an additional $36 billion. Who makes the money? Not the author. Retailers take almost 50%. The agent takes 15% to 20%. The publisher gets squeezed – it's cause for huge celebration if they make 20%. 'On a book that costs $24.95, the author gets at most $1 to $1.50,' says Eileen Gittins, chief executive of Blurb, an online print-on-demand publisher of photography books."*

It is certainly not my intent to bring the mood down here, but I want to give you a realistic portrayal of what people who attempt this route are facing. I know writers that have literally spent ten years trying to break into the world of traditional publishing. They work, they polish, they submit, they fret, they re-write, they re-submit, they continue to fret, and so on. The world of traditional publishing is a tough nut to crack, especially with the national publishing houses... and if you do, the payoff simply isn't there in most cases.

That's not your only option, though. I'd be remiss if I didn't mention that there are university presses, regional presses, and small presses that all do varying forms of traditional publishing. The fact that these are smaller operations can increase your odds of publication slightly, but you may be giving up promotional and distribution opportunities, since their staff and funds are much more limited than the larger houses. My advice? Well, keep reading before you make any decisions; I think that there are other aspects of the publishing world that you should consider.

Vanity Presses

Heaven protect us all from vanity presses! If you're thinking about using a vanity press, I have only one piece of advice... RUN AWAY! I'm serious – run like your rear end is on fire and the only pond is a mile away.

If that sounds harsh, well, first let me make a clear distinction between vanity presses and self-publishing… and there is a major one.

Vanity presses have always preyed on authors, making elaborate promises, taking their money, and doing little more than putting a few books in their hands. I have known more than an author or two who have been lured into these promises:
- "Your book will be published!"
- "It will be sold nationally!"
- "You can buy as many copies as you'd like to sell on your own!"

But what happens? You are required to pay a subsidiary fee for the privilege of your book being published, and it could be $1000, $1500 or more. At the end of the day, you're literally paying for your book to be published, with a nice, fat percentage added on for the vanity press. These places also offer selling packages and services, but the reality is that the only marketing for your book will be what you do for yourself. The only real advantage that you're gaining with a vanity press is that they know the exact process to get a book published... but those are the very things that this book teaches you, so why not cut out the extra layer of cash that you're paying the vanity press? That's exactly what I want you to do. We'll talk more about that in a bit, though. For now, keep in mind that if a publisher wants you to pay a single penny for your book to be published, they are a vanity press. I'm teaching you to know everything that they know, and do everything that they do, so there's no need to throw any money away on them.

Electronic Publishing

Ah, the thing that strikes fear into the heart of all publishing houses in America... electronic publishing!

This has been a worrisome thought for traditional publishers for years, because if it ever does take off with consumers, it could change the face of the industry forever. While some informational electronic books (ebooks) have prospered, ebooks of fiction, poetry, etc. have historically floundered.

In the last decade there have been several portable ebook readers that have hit the market, all that had one or more problems that plagued them. Just a few of these issues were:
- Some had no backlit screen, making the reader hard to use in dark places – in bed, on airplanes at night when the lights are dimmed, etc.

- Most were susceptible to environmental conditions; sand, humidity, water, heat and cold affected them, limiting the places where they could be used.
- Each had their own format for the ebooks, so that not every ebook would work on every reader. A few readers used HTML, others used PDF, and several had proprietary formats.
- Major publishers didn't want to start down the slippery-slope of electronic publishing, so few mainstream titles were made available.

These are just a few of the problems that electronic readers of the past decade faced, but there were many more. For ebooks to springboard into the mainstream world, a reader is going to have to address all those issues and overcome them. The answer may have already shown itself, however, in the form of Amazon.com's Kindle.

As of this writing, the Kindle has been designed to do several brilliant things – not only does it display ebooks, but it also accesses the web so that the reader can display everything from newspapers to magazines to blogs. Ebooks can be immediately downloaded straight from Amazon, making it extremely convenient. At the moment, over 120,000 titles have been made available for Kindle – and Amazon has even developed a tool to painlessly allow publishers to convert their titles for its use.

The consumer response has been overwhelming. For months, the Kindle was perpetually sold out, even though it sells for $400.00. Demand has literally overrun the supply, something that the industry is keeping a watchful eye on. Probably the most telling factor is that many major publishers are now making their titles available. In fact, about 90% of the current New York Times Best Sellers can be immediately downloaded to Kindle.

If you remember the Forbes article by Sramana Mitra titled, "How Amazon Could Change Publishing" that I mentioned earlier, it directly addresses Amazon's Kindle by saying: "Some surveys suggest that online booksellers could become the largest channel for book sales by 2009, and Amazon is certainly the 800-pound gorilla in that market – it's the largest bookseller in the world. To understand why, you have to look at the technology that powers Amazon's Web site. Yes, Amazon offers the best prices, but what really keeps customers coming back is the outstanding user experience. It was made possible by Amazon's acquisition of a small technology company Junglee in 1998. Junglee, which powers Amazon's now-famous recommendation system, uses a technology called collaborative filtering to figure out what other books people will like. It's a fantastic way to market and merchandise with contextual and personalized offers that can have a direct impact on the promotion of a particular book. Amazon has years of data on all its loyal customers and it consistently produces great recommendations. We reward Amazon with our wallets.

Amazon's ability to market books efficiently makes it wildly attractive as a channel, and the company knows it. Its recent moves shine some light on where its ambitions may lie. In 2005, it acquired the print-on-demand company BookSurge and Mobipocket.com, an e-book software company. In November, it launched the e-book reader Kindle. (According to Citigroup analyst Mark Mahaney, Kindle could contribute 3% of Amazon's overall revenue in two years.)

Amazon is poised to revolutionize the book printing business through vertical integration. Let's look at the numbers. Assuming that Amazon already pockets 50% of the retail price of a book, it could directly engage with authors and cut out the middlemen: the agent and the publisher. That would free up 30% to 40% of the pie, which can easily be split between Amazon and the author. Let's say, in the new world, Amazon becomes the retailer, marketer, publisher and agent combined and takes 65% of the revenues, offering 35% to the author – we end up with a much better, fairer world."

Will ebooks eventually take over the printed word? Of course – but probably not in our lifetime. Still, it looks like e-publishing becomes a more viable alternative every day – and we'll all be watching Amazon to see what happens with Kindle.

New Technology Publishers

This is another avenue of publishing that scares the living daylights out of traditional publishing houses. As technology improves, the publishing world continues to change.

Imagine this: you walk into a major bookstore chain, and they have shelves filled with books… only one copy of every title. You shop around, flip through many books, , and finally make a selection. Taking the book to a barcode scanner on the aisle, you pass it over the reader, and you return it to the shelf. Behind the counter, a machine kicks into gear, and in only a moment a copy of the book that you selected pops out – freshly printed on good quality paper with a beautiful, four-color cover. At the same time, your invoice is printed at the register, and you're immediately ready to go with your book in hand. Does that sound like a scene from some science fiction world? Well, to be honest, it's not all that far away.

Today, you can find a printer with a digital press where you can upload your file in PDF format, and they will do short runs of the book for a relatively low cost. For example, if you're using a printer with a traditional offset press, you may have to order 1,000 copies of a book to get it down to a manageable cost of $4 per item. In today's world, you can find a printer that can give you only 25 copies for $5 each, which relieves you of the pressure of a large initial investment, and finding a place to warehouse a thousand books.

Now, before you get too excited about the low cost, keep in mind that the book has to be ready to print. It has to be written, edited, and then put through the layout process. The cover has to be designed; all of that must be converted to a format that the printer's equipment can read, and then it must be uploaded to their server. The most common way to upload files is by using something called the File Transfer Protocol (FTP). Fortunately, there are programs that make FTP as easy as dropping and dragging files like you do on your computer.

The most important thing to keep in mind, though, is that anyone can overcome any of those obstacles that I mentioned just by reading this book, and can then afford to produce a book and hold it in his or her hand. The question at that point becomes: how are you going to sell it? Hold on to that thought, because we're going to address it a little bit later. For now, just consider the fact that a book can be cheaply produced, and that it is well within your grasp. This goes hand-in-hand with the next section that I want to talk about, because these new technology publishers, also known as print-on-demand or POD publishers, will make something wonderful available to you... the world of self-publishing.

Self-Publishing

Knowing the title of this book, you may not be surprised to discover that this is the option that I'm going to recommend for you. In years past, self-publishing was one of those things that was looked down upon – so much so that you had to carefully hide the fact that you'd published your own book. It was the kind of thing that you simply didn't talk about in polite company... not to your friends, not to your family, not to booksellers, and certainly not to other authors!

Why? Well, having a self-published book was a symbol to the industry that your book simply wasn't good enough to be traditionally published. It often meant that you'd exhausted all possible means of standard publication, and just given up. Face it; in the eyes of most people in the publishing world, being self-published meant that you were sub-standard, that you just weren't good enough. When writers gathered, self-published authors were shunned like lepers.

The problem that bookstores and distributors had with self-published books was that it often meant that the book was going to be poorly designed and written. In days of old, self-published authors seldom had editors polish their manuscripts, and so the books were more than a little rough.

It's a different world out there today, though. Pioneers in the self-publishing world have produced mega-hits like *The Bridges of Madison County* and *The Celestine Prophecy*, books whose sheer magnitude of sales simply can't be ignored. When I say that the world is changing, I mean that literally. If you remember the opening quote from the Forbes article that I quoted earlier, "Technology has disrupted every industry. Now, it's book publishing's turn." How has technology changed other industries? Look at just a couple of examples that immediately turned the world upside down.

Everyone is familiar with the recording artist Prince, who has been a major force in pop culture for the past few decades. In June of 2007, he was set to release his *Planet Earth* CD, but to launch it, he bypassed the distributors, the music stores, and anyone else who typically takes a cut of his music. He cut a deal with the major British newspaper "The Mail on Sunday" to include a free copy of his CD with their Sunday paper – although details of the arrangement are secret, speculation is that his fee was about what he would have received after the distributors and stores took their share of a first release… a price that was easily within reach of the newspaper. No one had ever been so arrogant in the face of the distributors and stores before, but it worked out to be not only financially lucrative for Prince, but he also received a ton of publicity over it… and it sent a shiver through the music publishing business.

That same year, the rock band The Eagles shook the foundations of the music publishing industry once again. For their new "Long Road Out Of Eden" album, the band members themselves paid to have it recorded, mixed and produced – and then signed an exclusive deal with Wal Mart to be the only place in the world to buy the album. Guess what – it still went to #1 on the charts! As of this writing, you can't even buy it retail from Amazon – only from Wal Mart. The music publishers and distributors are still reeling. If this trend continues, they would be completely and totally out of business. Can you imagine the closed-door boardroom meetings that took place over the Eagles' new album?

The entertainment industry is in crisis, including the book publishing world. The opportunity has never been better for individuals to launch their own product into the mainstream. That's not going to happen for everyone, though – it will take a lot of work and planning. The fact that the opportunity exists is exciting, though, and for authors, "new technology publisher" from the last section is what makes it possible.

As long as we're talking about taking advantage of self publishing, we should spend some time looking at the various aspects of producing you own book. Ready? Let's dive in.

BOOK DESIGN

Know what I love to do? Plumbing.

That's right, I'm an amateur plumber. I don't know much about the local building codes, but if there's a water problem in my house that can be addressed with PVC pipe, then I can probably handle it.

Not long ago a friend asked me to help add a bathroom to his house, and after looking at the job, I realized that this was larger than anything I'd ever attempted. There would be issues with how far apart the drain connections were, how the system would be vented, and so forth. I could have picked up a guidebook and waded in, but I knew that a job of this magnitude had to be done right, and that my friend would be living with the results for a very long time. If I don't know anything else, I hope that I know when I'm in over my head, and it's time to call in a pro. We called in a plumber to do the work, and I've never regretted that decision.

The exact same thing is true when it comes to book design – be very clear on what you can do yourself, and what you need to bring in a professional to do. Once the book is complete, you'll have it for a very long time, and you want it to be the best that it possibly can be. Whether you hire out the different aspects of your book, or you have the talent to do them yourself, you'll need to be familiar with several aspects of book publishing – copyright, ISBNs, LCCNs, bleed, justification, widows/orphans, paper weight, etc. We'll cover those items in this section to help you gain an understanding of them.

COPYRIGHT

Before we get into the meat of this chapter, let me make one thing perfectly clear: I'm not an attorney, and therefore I am not qualified to dispense legal advice when it comes to copyright law (or any other legal topic such as marriage, divorce, or traffic tickets, for that matter). What I can provide you are my opinions based upon my own experiences in the publishing world, and conventional wisdom gathered over the years from the industry. That said, let's talk a little about copyright.

Here's the basic fact that you need to know about it: with today's laws, and by that I mean that if you have created your work after January 1, 1978, once you've done so you automatically own the copyright to it. Write a paragraph describing the sunset, and you own it. Snap a photo, and you own it. Paint a picture, you own that as well. You aren't required to register it anywhere, or do anything else – you automatically own the copyright to anything you create. You can reproduce the work yourself, or assign the copyright to someone else via contract for that person or entity to use the work.

Now, you can certainly register your creation with the government copyright office – it only costs $20 – and if doing so will give you peace of mind, then by all means I encourage you to do it. The instructions are easy to follow, and the price is certainly reasonable. Just go to: **http://www. copyright.gov/register/.** Registering your copyrighted material does give you some legal protection should there ever be a challenge, and it will allow you to sue for copyright infringement (or protect yourself against it). There are a few things that I want to you know about copyright in general, though.

The first is that your work is already fairly secure – unless you post it in its entirety online, no one will likely steal it. And even if you did that, chances are that unscrupulous website builders would harvest portions of your work for their own website content. In the real world, it is unlikely that someone will steal your entire work and publish it as their own.

As far as getting it copyrighted to keep someone from publishing it under their own name, it is very, very rare that anything like that happens. Some people are certain that this is going to occur, though, and go to all kinds of lengths to prevent it... but most of the time, it only makes them look amateurish. For example, I heard a literary agent speak at a writer's conference, and she said that any author with copyright mania became an instant joke around their office. Occasionally, someone would send in a manuscript for consideration of representation, and in both the introductory letter and on the front of the manuscript there would be a paragraph that said something like: "NOTICE: The copyright on this work has been registered with the United States Government, and any attempt to steal it will be prosecuted to the fullest extent of the law!!!" Furthermore, these type manuscripts would include the name of the work and the © symbol on every single page in the header or footer, and include any other notifications to fully demonstrate that the writer was bordering on obsession with the whole issue of copyright. The agent said that after everyone got a good laugh, they'd simply toss the entire packet in the trash, assuming that the writer would be too much of a pain to work with, no matter what the quality of the manuscript was.

If you want to try to get your work traditionally published, there is absolutely no reason to make a big deal out of the copyright. Editors, agents, publishers and printers all know that it is your work and will respect that fact.

If you are producing the book yourself, then the only mention that you will need to make is on the copyright page, which will look something like this:

That's really all that you need to do – your book is protected at that point, and it would be an extremely rare occurrence for someone to try to publish it under their own name... it just doesn't happen.

Another concept that you need to understand is that copyright protects an exact work, not an idea; in fact, ideas can't be copyrighted at all. Let's use the example of a photograph for a moment – imagine that you and I both happen to be visiting San Francisco at the same time. You pull your car into the south observation point parking lot just as I do, and we each get out of our respective vehicles and walk over to the spot looking out over the bay, with a dramatic view of the bridge and the city of San Francisco in the background. Standing side by side, we each find ourselves in awe of the incredible landscape before us, and then simultaneously raise our cameras, and snap that beautiful picture. Essentially, we each have the exact same photograph in our camera, but you own the copyright on yours, and I own the copyright on mine. You can sell yours to a travel magazine, and I can do the same with mine... and neither of us have violated each other's copyrights.

Now turn that example into the writing world. Let's say that you wrote a book on touring the Grand Canyon. I pick it up in a store, read it, and decide that I want to do a book on the same topic. If I did my own research, and write my own book in my own words, then there wouldn't be a copyright infringement – even though you might not be happy about the fact that I wrote it.

The bottom line is this – you cannot copyright an idea, just a specific work. When the Chicken Soup for the Soul® series came out with the success that it did, there were many imitators that immediately released similar books to try to ride the wave. Many fell by the wayside, but a few are still hanging around doing their own series.

I've spent the last page or so giving some varied aspects of the copyright issue, but it all boils down to this – there is seldom, if ever, a problem that you're going to encounter. If you create the work, you own the copyright automatically. If you publish the work, put the copyright page in the book as shown above. If it makes you feel safer, then go ahead and spend the twenty bucks to register it. No matter what, though, if you created the work on and after January 1, 1978, the law says that the copyright term for works created by an individual is the life of the author plus 50 years. Chances are, when the copyright term is set to expire, you won't be a bit worried about it anyway… you will have passed away fifty years before!

THE LIBRARY OF CONGRESS CONTROL NUMBER

Depending on the age of the reference that you're reading (or the person that you're talking to) you may hear the Library of Congress book identification numbers – the LCCN – referred to as the "Library of Congress Card Number," the "Library of Congress Card Catalog Number," or even the "Library of Congress Control Number." They all refer to the same thing – a unique number assigned to each Library of Congress catalog record. The LCCN has always referred to the number associated with the bibliographic record created by the Library of Congress, or any other library, for a particular book.

In years past, an actual printed card in a card catalog was the most popular format for displaying the bibliographic record of a book – you may remember that at one time every library had a huge, wooden cabinet containing an index card record for every book there. Because of this, the number associated with the book's card record was commonly referred to as the "Library of Congress Card Number" or the "Library of Congress Card Catalog Number."

Like everything else in our world, libraries have evolved and now use online systems to catalog books, instead of the old paper cards. The LCCN, while still serving the purpose of identifying a book's bibliographic record, is now referred to as the "Library of Congress Control Number."

Now let me add one more acronym, hopefully without confusing things any worse. There is also something called a PCN, which stands for "Pre-assigned Control Number." A PCN is nothing more than a LCCN that has been assigned to a book before it has been published. This helps out a publisher, because the LCCN can then be printed in the front of the book starting with the very first edition.

Now, while this may be good background knowledge for you, there's still probably a question in the back of your mind about why in the world you would need an LCCN, especially if you are going to self-publish a book targeted toward a specific audience. Take the example that we've used in the past, about the mechanic who wants to write a book for his customers – would it benefit him to have a Library of Congress Control Number for his book? On the surface I'd probably say "no," but there are a couple of points for his book... as well as yours.

The first thing to consider is that you really don't know what is going to happen with your book. While you may never consider it being placed in a library, what if it became a runaway best-seller? Although it may not be likely, you have to admit that there is always a possibility. If your book is already set up for success, then you're ahead of the game... and I'm going to make that exact same argument for getting an ISBN for it in just a few moments.

The other item to mention about LCCNs is that it just helps the book look, well, professional. I'm certain that you've probably picked up one or more books in your life that just didn't look, well, *right*. Maybe it was that it didn't have the copyright page, or there wasn't a bar code on back, or any number of little things that seem to scream, "SELF-PUBLISHED!!!" With a LCCN on the copyright page, the words "Library of Congress Control Number" just seem to give the book a little official weight.

One final point that I want to mention – the LCCN is free, and to be honest, how long has it been since you've gotten something free from the government? Actually, that is not exactly true – when your book is published, you are required to send one copy to the Library of Congress. Other than that, you don't have to pay a cent. To get set up for your PCN application, just go to the website:

http://pcn.loc.gov/

Click on "Open New Account" to get started, and then every time that you need to register for a new LCN, just go back and click on "Log On." It takes 1-2 weeks for you to receive your account username and password, and 1-2 weeks to get the PCN via email. Once the book is printed, you will send a copy of it by U.S. Postal Service to:

Library of Congress
Cataloging in Publication Division
101 Independence Avenue, S.E.
Washington, D.C. 20540-4320

It's as easy as that, and will greatly help the professional appearance of your book.

ISBNs

The International Standard Book Number (ISBN) is a 13-digit number that identifies a particular book. It is quite a important little number – it allows bookstores to index their books and order more when they're out, to locate and contact the publisher, and to even scan the ISBN barcodes to correlate books to prices, and coordinate automatic inventory control.

The ISBN breaks down into several parts:
- A country identifier that indicates the national origin of the publisher
- A publisher identifier that is specific to the publisher of the book
- A title identifier specific to the book within the publisher's catalog
- A check digit is the single digit at the end of the ISBN which validates it

Much like LCCNs, you may wonder why it is necessary for your book to have an ISBN, especially if you are going to only be distributing it directly to your clients, or at the back of the room when you are speaking. I would make the same argument that I did for LCCNs… what's that old saying? "If it walks like a duck, and it quacks like a duck, then it must be a duck." If your book has all the same things as a New York publication, then people will perceive it as just as professional an item.

There is another more tangible reason, though. Should you decide to make the book publicly available, most bookstores, online sellers (Amazon.com, bn.com, etc), and distributors will not handle a book without an ISBN that is printed inside the book and on the back cover with a barcode. This alone is a good reason to obtain one for your book.

This will cost you over a hundred bucks, so it isn't as cheap as registering a copyright ($20) or getting a LCCN (free). The decision is strictly yours, and it is one that you have to make before going too much farther. If you print 1,000 copies of your book without an ISBN, then it's too late to change your mind. On the other hand, if you have worked out your sales and distribution model and you are certain that the book won't be on stores – online or at the mall – then you probably won't need one.

The ISBN is something that must be applied for… so who can apply for an ISBN? Well, according to the official ISBN website, "The ISBN Agency assigns ISBNs at the direct request of publishers, e-book publishers, audio cassette and video producers, software producers and museums and associations with publishing programs."

So who can get an ISBN? Well, I'm sorry to be the bearer of bad news, but basically, only publishers can. Yep, your book won't have an ISBN unless it has a publisher…

...unless you form your own publishing house! Sound daunting? Actually, it's not that bad at all, and we're going to talk about that next. You might be surprised how easy it is, and what benefits it carries. Before jumping into that, however, here are the prices for an ISBN:

1 ISBN	$125.00
10 ISBNs	$370.00
100 ISBNs	$1,055.00
1000 ISBNs	$1,695.00

If you only need one ISBN, it will cost you $125. If you think that you'll be doing multiple books, however, it is a much better deal to buy ten of them for $370 – purchasing them separately would cost $1,250, so you would save $880! Of course, you would probably never need a thousand ISBNs, but purchasing 10 is something to consider – if you end up publishing three books, then it is a very economical option.

Once you are a "publishing entity," then it is relatively easy to sign up with the U.S. ISBN agency, and then apply for the ISBNs. Simply go to: **www.isbn.org.** There you can follow the step-by-step instructions, and before you know it, you'll have a list of ISBNs at your disposal.

I have to mention that there is one thing that drives me crazy. Now, this isn't part of the education that you're receiving from the book, or even something that you'll ever have to worry about... I just need to rant a moment. I can't stand it when people refer to these book identifiers as "ISBN Numbers." In effect, to say that, you are saying "International Standard Book Number Numbers." It's the same way that many people refer to those money-dispensing devices as "ATM Machines" – which in essence means "Automatic Teller Machine Machines." Okay, okay, I know that I'm just rambling here, but I want you to sound professional when talking about these numbers. Plus, when someone mentions "ISBN Numbers" to you, it's fun to look at them with a puzzled expression and say, "So, are you talking about International Standard Book Number Numbers?" Of course, that may just be something that I enjoy with my sense of humor, but I couldn't resist passing it on to you.

I guess that's enough frivolity – it's time to talk about something serious… forming your own publishing house. Sound daunting? Sound expensive? Actually, it's neither, and I'm going to share all the details with you. Read on…

FORMING YOUR OWN PUBLISHING HOUSE

Like I said, this sounds like an arduous task. Forming your own Publishing House? It must be a tedious, expensive proposition. From the sound of it you will probably have to fly to New York, find some expensive office space, rent a warehouse, start interviewing employees, and bring in printing presses to round out your price tag at a few million bucks. Right?

Wrong! I'm going to give you the formula right now that will make you a legitimate (although small) press. Are you ready? Good – here's what you have to do.

1. Choose a name. This is the hardest part of the entire process, though. First of all, don't make it anything connected to your personal name. For example, if your name is John Doe, DO NOT name your publishing house "John Doe Press," or even "Doe Press." If you do that, and someone sees that your book is by "John Doe," then it doesn't take a rocket scientist to figure out that the book is self-published through your own press. By the same token, don't select something that sounds too corporate – if your publishing house is named "International Conglomerate Publishing," then it probably won't be taken seriously. Simple names are better, like some that I've seen along the way: "Solstice Press," "Saturday House," "October Moon Press," etc. If you want to make sure that your name isn't taken, just go to: **www.google. com** and do a search for the name that you selected, enclosed in quotes. If someone else is using that name in any manner, you will find it. You definitely want to be unique. One more thing – go to a domain registration site such as 000domains.com and search for a web site domain name with the publishing house name you're considering. For example, do a search for solsticepress. com, saturdayhouse.com, or octobermoonpress.com – whatever name you're considering. If it is available, pay the small price to register the domain; you're going to use it later.

2. Once you've selected a moniker for the press, then you must register it as a business name. Check with your county courthouse for the details, because it can vary from place to place. A good friend of mine just did this, and all he had to do was to go down to the courthouse and check the online records to verify that no one else had his business name, then fill out a simple form, and finally attach a check for $25. After that, he was a business. These things vary by state and by county, so your registration may be free, it may cost $100, or it may only be twenty-five bucks like it was for my friend. At that point, however, guess what? You're a publishing house! Done deal – that's the basic thing that you have to do.

3. In case you're going to get checks to your publishing house instead of your personal name, you may want to do a bit of financial finagling. The courthouse will give you some paperwork that you can take to your bank to file a "DBA," or "Doing Business As" form. This just tells the powers that be – the IRS and the State Comptroller – that any business conducted by your publishing house name is linked back to you. This is an important step, because it is imperative that you run your business above board and in accordance with all applicable laws and procedures. The other thing that it does, though, is allow you to take checks and payments made to your publishing house name. The bigger your business becomes, the more important this is.

4. You'll probably want to get a web page so that you'll have an internet presence. It doesn't have to be anything more than an introductory page, but in today's world any legitimate business has a website. A little mom-and-pop kitchen products store three

blocks away from me has its own website – everyone does! Of course, I could put together a book twice the size of this one describing all the aspects of getting a site on the web. Instead, though, I'd bet that you know someone with web experience that can help you get a simple, professional web site established. Here's a secret, though: if you don't have a friend that does, I'd be willing to be that you have a friend who has a son or daughter that can get a web page up for you in a second! That shouldn't surprise you, because kids today are an order of magnitude more technical than any of us have ever aspired to be. Just be careful – there are many website-building services that can charge hundreds – if not thousands – of dollars to get a site up and running. Start with a simple, basic website and go from there. The bottom line is this: get your domain name registered, and get a website up.

5. Finally, you may want to consider getting a SAN – a Standard Address Number. According to the agency's website, the SAN is described as follows:

The Standard Address Number (SAN) is a unique seven-digit identifier used to signify a specific address of an organization in (or served by) the publishing industry. It is an American National Standard, ANSI/NISO Z39.43-1993.

This system, initiated and maintained by R.R. Bowker, has become THE identification code for electronic communication within the industry.

It is the method used by PUBNET, X*NET and PubEasy. com systems and is required in all electronic data interchange communications using the Book Industry Systems Advisory Committee (BISAC) EDI formats.

The SAN itself has no functional meaning -- it merely defines an address. The SAN becomes meaningful only when used for identification of customers for electronic ordering transmission, voice recognition ordering systems, tele-ordering, for billing or shipping account numbers, etc.

The use of the SAN significantly reduces the problems faced by other non-standard numbering systems such as billing errors, books shipped to the wrong points, errors in payments and returns.

Entities using the SAN include book and journal publishers, wholesalers and distributors, book retailers and college bookstores, libraries, schools and universities, as well as paper and cloth manufacturers, printers and binders and others involved in the manufacturing of books and journals.

What does all that mean? Well, it comes down to two things: 1) if someone in the bookselling industry wants to contact you, it gives them an avenue to do so; and 2) it looks official to everyone who sees your publishing house named followed by a SAN – like I keep saying, if it walks like a duck and it quacks like a duck, then it must be a duck. To sign up for a SAN, go to: **www.isbn.com** and click on the SAN link at the top of the page. All the information that you need will be there.

As you can see, there isn't a single aspect of forming your own publishing house that is tough to overcome. It is a simple process, and can not only give your books a more prestigious appearance, but will also allow you to apply for ISBNs.

Whether you decide to form a publishing house or not, though, you still have a book to produce, and we're going to launch into that topic next.

BOOK LAYOUT

We discussed editing back in the last chapter, so at this point we'll assume that the book is done. You may have an ISBN, you may have your own publishing house, but the important thing is that you have a complete manuscript that is ready for publication. The first step is to have the book layout done. In the old days this was called "typesetting," but in our world today it simply means that you turn the manuscript over to a professional who can lay out the book and get it ready for printing.

The temptation may be there to take a stab at this step yourself, but it is a lot like the editing process – a little upfront money paid to a professional will give your book a polished appearance. It can be an extremely complicated process, even in a book that looks relatively simple. For example, I was recently discussing this subject with a layout artist that I use. He just finished working on a book that was about 250 pages, and in flipping through it, you would consider it to look like most any book on a store's shelf. The magnitude of the job was incredible, though. There were sixty chapters, and each one had to be defined as a separate section. Within each section there were different headers for the first page, the left page, and the right page. Page numbering in the footer had to continue from the previous section and pass smoothly into the next one, except for the sections that were part of the front matter, which had their own numbering system. Each section had to have margins and a gutter defined, and widows/orphans had to be managed. Add to that justification issues, tables, illustrations, and index and special fonts, and the job took many man-hours to complete. I tell you this not to overwhelm you, but instead to demonstrate the reason that you will probably want to consider using a professional.

There are several things to consider about your book's layout, and although your layout artist will be familiar with them, you will need to be able to talk about them. Here are some of the major ones:

Size – the average book size for a trade paperback is 8.5 inches tall by 5.5 inches wide. While you will see odd-sized books, my advice is to stick to the industry standard.

Margins – as you may already have guessed, this is the distance of the block of words from each edge of the page. Margins can vary, but a good rule of thumb is to use the following specifications:

Edge	Margin
Top	.5"
Bottom	.75"
Left	.5"
Right	.5"

Margins must be consistent throughout the book, but do be aware that there is one other factor related to margins: the gutter.

Gutter – this is an easy concept to grasp; when you open the pages of any book, you'll notice that some space is lost on the inside edges of each page where they are bound to the spine of the book. Because of this, in the layout process a little extra space must be allocated for the binding; this extra space is known as the "gutter." Typically the gutter only needs to be a quarter of an inch (.25"), but this little extra space is important to the appearance of your book.

Font – The font that is used in your book can be problematic if not handled correctly. Filling the book with many different fonts will make it extremely difficult to read, because the reader will be distracted. The different fonts used in the book become the focus, instead of the material itself. If you go to your local bookstore and thumb through most any book on the shelf, you will find that the book uses "Times New Roman" 12-point font. It's an industry standard, and one to which you should adhere. There is another, more technical issue, however – the fonts that are on your computer will not necessarily be on the printer's computer. If you use a fancy curlicue font that doesn't exist on your printer's computer, some random font will be substituted and all formatting will be skewed. If you are using any special fonts, make sure that when your book is converted to PDF format (more on that later) the actual fonts that you use are "imbedded" in the document. This is an option in the PDF conversion process that must be set in advance, and your layout person will know how to do it.

Chapter Headings – The one exception to the Times New Roman font rule is that of Chapter Headings and the Title Page. You may want to select a different font to accent those items… and *just* those items. That means you will have used only two fonts for your book: Times New Roman for the body, and one other font for the title/headings. At this point, it becomes crucial for the fonts to be imbedded during the PDF conversion process – this places the font information physically in the PDF file, so that the book will look the same no matter what computer platform it is presented on, and whether or not that computer has those individual font files.

Headers – these are the areas at the top of every page where some books put the chapter titles, book title, section title, etc. Once again, visit your local bookstore and flip through several different books. I keep asking you to do that, I know, but there is no better way to get information than to look at examples – and your local bookstore is full of them! There are three different headers to consider when you're looking at those example books:

- First Page Heading – this is the heading of the first page of every section or chapter. Many times the header of the chapter title page is blank, so that the heading will not detract from the title. The First Page Heading supersedes any other heading information; for example, if it happens to fall on the left-hand page, that page will use the first page heading instead of the left page heading.
- Even Page Heading – this is the heading that will appear on every left-hand page. Some books will have the book title appear on every left-hand page.
- Odd Page Heading – this is the heading that will appear on every right-hand page. You will see books that have the chapter title appear on the right-hand pages.

There is no particular standard for the headers. When you're looking through all the books at your bookstore, just make note of those that catch your eye, and that represent how you want your book to appear.

Footers – These are much like the headers that we just talked about. If footers are used, they are usually reserved just for page numbers. Occasionally the page numbers appear on the headers, and in that case, the footers are usually blank.

Page Numbering – as long as we're talking about page numbers, I'm sure that you're familiar with the standard numbering scheme, but I wanted to mention it here just for completeness. The first few pages of the book – title page, copyright page, dedication, etc. – typically don't have any page numbers. When you start the table of contents, table of figures/illustrations, and other such pages you should use Roman numerals starting with one (i, ii, iii, iv, v, and so forth). On the first page of chapter one, start the numbering over again with a decimal one (1, 2, 3, 4, 5, etc.) and continue this throughout the book. It probably goes without saying that you should use the automatic page numbering feature of your word processing program – do not use insert them manually! To do so is a recipe for disaster, because during the editing process the pagination will change drastically, and you want the page numbers to change automatically.

Justification – this refers to the alignment of words on the page. Most word processors offer four different options: left justified, right justified, centered, and even margins. Here are examples of each:

Left Justified:
"While we were at the Tejas village, after we had distributed clothing to the Indians and to the governor of the Tejas, the said governor asked me one evening for a piece of blue baize to make a shroud in which to bury his

mother when she died. I told him that cloth would be more suitable, and he answered that he did not want any color other than blue."

Right Justified:

"While we were at the Tejas village, after we had distributed clothing to the Indians and to the governor of the Tejas, the said governor asked me one evening for a piece of blue baize to make a shroud in which to bury his mother when she died. I told him that cloth would be more suitable, and he answered that he did not want any color other than blue."

Centered:

"While we were at the Tejas village, after we had distributed clothing to the Indians and to the governor of the Tejas, the said governor asked me one evening for a piece of blue baize to make a shroud in which to bury his mother when she died. I told him that cloth would be more suitable, and he answered that he did not want any color other than blue."

Even Margins:

"While we were at the Tejas village, after we had distributed clothing to the Indians and to the governor of the Tejas, the said governor asked me one evening for a piece of blue baize to make a shroud in which to bury his mother when she died. I told him that cloth would be more suitable, and he answered that he did not want any color other than blue."

The default for most word processors is almost always left justified, but for your book, you should really do even, justified margins. It is the industry standard, and doing anything else will make your book amateurish. This can be done during the book layout process, but be aware that it can change the pagination considerably.

Widows/Orphans – in the publishing world, widows and orphans are those words or short phrases at the end or beginning of paragraphs that are left to sit alone at the top or bottom of a page, separated from the rest of the paragraph. After your book has gone through the layout phase, you will probably find several widows and orphans that need to be corrected. Unfortunately, there is only way to fix widows and orphans – the text of the chapter must be edited. Here is a trick to remember, though, that will make the process much easier. Let's look at an example of two pages to illustrate it:

It had been a long winter of traveling through the extreme wilderness, and the company was becoming restless.

While we were at the Tejas village, after we had distributed clothing to the Indians and to the governor of the Tejas, the said governor asked me one evening for a piece of blue baize to make a shroud in which to bury his mother when she died. I told him that cloth would be more suitable, and he answered that he did

33

not want any color other than blue.

34

If these were two pages from your book, you can see that there is an orphan line, "not want any color other than blue." That needs to be pulled up to the preceding page. That means that you have to edit seven words out of the paragraph to make the change. If you look up to the paragraph above it, though, there is a line containing only the word "restless." It would be much easier to remove one word from that paragraph that to remove seven from the next. In fact, if you take out the word "extreme" you haven't change the meaning of the text that much, and everything ends on the page just like you'd want:

> *It had been a long winter of traveling through the wilderness, and the company was becoming restless.*
>
> *While we were at the Tejas village, after we had distributed clothing to the Indians and to the governor of the Tejas, the said governor asked me one evening for a piece of blue baize to make a shroud in which to bury his mother when she died. I told him that cloth would be more suitable, and he answered that he did not want any color other than blue.*
>
> *33*

Keep that little trick in mind when you're fixing widows/orphans. Look back through the chapter, and find a paragraph with the minimum number of words on the last line – that will be the one that you want to edit, because it will contain the least number of words to edit out.

Index – A rule of thumb: fiction books rarely have a back index, but non-fiction books almost always do. Just like page numbering, you should never put in your index by hand. If you were to hard-code all the page numbers in the index, and then you added one page during the layout process, it would throw every entry in the index completely off. Most word processors have a mechanism for automatically flagging words that should be added to the index. By using it, any shifting of page numbers will be handled and adjusted automatically.

PDF – although this acronym is thrown around a lot in the industry, very few people know that it actually stands for "Portable Document Format." It is a document-encoding process that was developed by the Adobe company that preserves document characteristics such as page layout, fonts, and graphics. Probably the most important aspect of PDF format is that it can be used across all different computer platforms: PC, Mac, Unix, etc. Most every professional printer can take a PDF file and print it as a book. Because of that, when you are contracting for book layout, make sure that in the end you will have a PDF file of your manuscript. Although users can download a free PDF reader from adobe. com, the package to convert word processing files to PDF (a program called "Acrobat Distiller") must be purchased separately, and can be quite expensive. When everything is said and done, however, your laid-out manuscript must be in PDF format.

COVER DESIGN

There's an old saying that "you can't judge a book by its cover." Know what? When it comes to selling books, that phrase is complete and total nonsense. In this world, you can definitely tell a book by its cover – at least, that is the way that consumers perceive it.

I'd be willing to bet that you (and everyone else who is reading this book) has walked into a bookstore and picked something up specifically because of the way that the cover looked. By the same token, I'd wager that you have seen books with very amateurish covers that you immediately dismiss. Consider these two covers...

Change
Your
Life
Now!

by John Doe

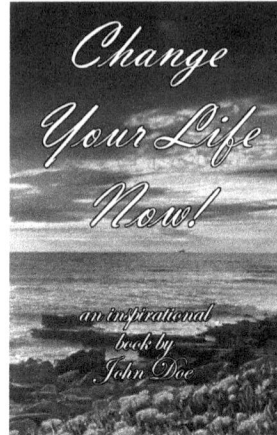

They're the same book, but one was done in a plain, straightforward cover, and the other that was laid out well using clouds and a sunrise. Glancing at both of them, which version of the book would you pick up in a bookstore?

Your book cover is that important – whether your book is in a store, or is on your table in the back of the room where you're speaking, people will judge it by the way it looks.

If you have an eye for layout, and you know how to use a graphics package such as Adobe Photoshop or Microsoft Visio, then it's altogether feasible that you can design your own cover. If not, then maybe you know someone who can help out: your spouse, a friend, or even an acquaintance at work. You can even hire a contractor that specializes in covers to handle it for you.

In any of these cases, there are a few things that you should understand about the business of book covers. The first is something called "bleed", which is basically an overlap of the borders. If your book is 8.5"x5.5" your printer may require a quarter inch bleed on every side. The cover that you send them would therefore include an extra .25 inch on each side, so the image that you send them would be 9"x6".

The next thing to consider is the type of book that you are thinking of printing – hardcover, pulp paperback, or trade paperback. Hardcover has extra expense, and trust me, you don't want to do a pulp paperback (a book the size of a romance or western novel), so the option that is most viable for your book would be a trade paperback, which is 8.5"x5.5". That is the format of the large majority of books that you'll find in any bookstore, and is what consumers have been conditioned to purchase.

Spine width is another crucial element in designing your book cover. If your calculation for the width is too narrow, then your front and back cover will offset into the spine. On the other hand, if the calculation is too wide, then it will push the front and back covers off the far edge of the book. Thankfully, most printers are very helpful to provide you information about spine width, so don't hesitate a moment to discuss it with your customer service representative there. To get an idea for yourself as to how thick your book will be, you can use a formula that is not a bit complicated. There are three variables that you will need:

1. The first thing that you need is the *exact* number of pages that your book will contain. Don't just go by the page numbers, because that will only indicate the number of

pages in the main body of the book. Let's say that your book, once it has been laid out and is in its final PDF form, has a final page number of 254. Add a page to the count for the main title page, another for the copyright page, another if you have a dedication page, one more if there is a blank page after it, and then one for each page of the table of contents (let's say two, for example). That means you have 254 + 1 title page + 1 copyright + 1 dedication + 1 blank + 2 table of contents = 260 total pages. Just to be perfectly clear, please understand that we are talking about pages you read, not physical sheets of paper; one piece of paper will contain two pages, a front and a back.

2. The second parameter that you will have to find out is the number of Pages Per Inch, or PPI. Your printer will be able to provide this to you based on the type of paper that you selected for your book. If you are using 50# (50-pound) paper, the PPI would be somewhere around 500. For 60# paper, it is more like 400 PPI. Because all paper varies slightly, to calculate the exact width you will need to get the precise PPI for your paper from the printer. We'll discuss the specifics of pound-weight of paper shortly, but for now just concentrate on the PPI.

3. Finally, you will need the thickness of the cover stock, which your printer can also provide you with. For example if your cover stock is 10 pt. C1S (ten-point, coating one-side – more about this later) its thickness might be .010 inch. Note that if you are producing a hardback book, the thickness will be much greater.

You can plug these three parameters into the following formula to determine the spine width of your book:

(# pages / PPI) + (2 * cover thickness) = spine width

For example, if you have 260 pages, a PPI of 400, and a cover thickness of .010, the result would be .67 inches, which was calculated as follows:

$$(260 / 400) + (2 * .010) = .67\ inches$$

Well, we've spent some time talking about some of the mechanics and specifications related to book cover design, so now let me give you some personal advice that I've found to be quite practical. Whether you are designing your cover yourself, or you are working with a friend or contractor to produce one, I can give you one hint that is going to help you immensely. Think about your book, how you want it to look, and how you want the cover to represent it. Next, go to a bookstore – preferably one of those big chains where they carry thousands and thousands of books (like I've suggested for inspiration in other parts of your book development). First visit the section of your book's genre, and start looking at covers. Jot down the names and authors of the ones that catch your eye, and then start expanding to related genres, all the while noting covers that catch your eye. This won't cost you a cent, and you can get many, many ideas for your own book cover.

PRINT YOUR BOOK

We've already talked about some of the different options that you have for printing your book, but no matter what you choose, there are some basic parameters that you're going to have to provide, so I want to close this section out with a discussion of them. These items will be invaluable when discussing your book with a printer, or with a publisher that is going to handle all the details for you. Here are the things that you will need to know:

Book Size

We touched on this earlier. You'll find people doing books ranging from 2"x3", to coffee table books that are 12"x14". The average, standard, American bookstore book is 8.5" high and 5.5" wide, however. Some people want to grab attention for their book by making it a different, odd size, but I would implore you to stick to the standard size. The printer is used to it, the distributor is used to it, the bookstores are used to it, and the consumers are *certainly* used to it.

Paper

In the Unites States, the weight of paper is expressed in pound-weight. You'll see this whether you're buying a package of inkjet printer paper at your local office supply store, or placing an order for your new book to be printed. Typical weights that you'll see are 20# (twenty-pound), 50#, 60#, 70#, etc. What this figure actually means is the weight in pounds of one ream (500 sheets) of uncut paper. The basic, uncut size of bond paper is 17 inches by 22 inches, or four times the size of standard 8.5" x 11" paper that you're used to seeing. A ream of 20# bond paper would weigh – you guessed it – twenty pounds. Out of this you could get 4 – 500-sheet packages of paper, each of which would weigh five pounds (20 pounds / 4 packages). You don't have to worry too much about all these calculations, though; just keep in mind two simple facts:

    1. The heavier the paper, the better the quality.
    2. The heavier the paper, the higher the price.

Most quality books have 60# paper, which is what I would recommend for your book. Authors who are trying to pinch pennies sometimes opt for 50# paper to save a little money, but in a quote that I received from one printer, there was only a difference of about twelve cents per book. If I was printing 100 books, then it would cost me only $12.00 more to have 60# paper instead of 50#. 1,000 books would be #120.00 more, which is starting to become a noticeable amount of money, but the difference in the way that your book will look and feel is well worth it. I've gone through this explanation so that you will understand paper weight and be able to discuss it intelligently, but my advice all boils down to this: use 60# paper.

Cover Stock

There are as many types of cover weights and finishes as there are types of paper. Printers will use a heavy stock that is laminated or coated on one side (the outside of the finished book). You'll see what I mean if you go pull any perfect-bound book off of your bookshelf; look at it and you will notice that the outside cover is probably glossy, while the inside cover is just plain unfinished paper. That type of cover is referred to as "coated, one side," or simply C1S for short. On a book where there is printing on the inside cover and it is finished in a glossy coating as well, the cover stock is called "coated, two sides" or C2S. The coating adds another feature to your book cover, however: it keeps it from curling! Cover curling is a bane of the publishing world, and your printer is fully aware of this fact. You should therefore discuss any such concerns with your customer service representative – it may be that the printer has some special cover treatments to offer that helps prevent curling.

The finishing on the cover stock can be glossy, matte, or any other type that the printer provides, but I would recommend a simple glossy finish. You'll probably find more books like that than with any other finish; it gives the book a strong, professional look.

Book Specifications

With everything that we've discussed, you should now be able to look at the specifications from any printer quote and understand exactly what each item means. Here is a real-life example of the specifications that came with a quote that I received from a printer:

- 5 1/2 (width) x 8 1/2 (height, spine)
- 242 pages
- perfect bound
- b&w interior on 60 lb white acid-free finch opaque vellum, 436 ppi, no bleeds (no printing within 3/8" edge of the page)
- 4-color cover on 10 pt. C1S with gloss lay flat lamination, bleeds (1/8" bleed and spine width must be included in file), cover prints 1 side only

Those specifications would produce a nice, professional book; it would be comparable to a book on the shelves produced by any major publishing house.

WAREHOUSING YOUR BOOK

You probably haven't given this a single thought, but when the printer ships the books to you, they must have a place to live. It can be in a warehouse that you've rented, in a corner of your garage, or even in a closet – but you have to plan ahead so that they're not stacked in a huge pyramid in the center of your living room.

Remember that your books are tangible assets. You have time and money invested in them, and you must protect them from harm. There are several things to worry about, but here are some of a book's most common enemies:

Water – If your books are stored in a building with a leaky roof, a simple rainstorm can destroy everything. On the other hand, you may have them stacked in a home closet that seems well-protected, but if a water heater were to burst and flood the area, the books would wick up the water like a stack of sponges and you would lose much of your stock. If you have several cases of books in stock, you may want to procure a wooden pallet that will keep them six inches off the ground at all times – no matter where they are stored, a simple pallet can protect from any flood or high water.

Fire – This goes without saying, and is probably not going to be one of your primary concerns. After all, in a lot of cases your books will be your least worries in a fire. If you store the books in your house somewhere and a fire breaks out, you'll be thinking about your family and pets instead. If you rent one of those "you-store-it" warehouses, they generally have metal walls and roofs, and concrete floors; the landlord has usually built a certain amount of fire-resistance into the place. Still, wherever you settle on to store your books, consider any potential fire hazards and make sure that they are at the lowest risk possible.

Extreme Temperature – I worried about keeping my books in a climate-controlled environment for a long time; but that was until I visited the warehouse of a large publisher. As one of the editors was walking me through the rows and rows of industrial-sized shelves stacked high with pallets of books, I was shocked that the building wasn't climate-controlled. Don't get me wrong; the books were protected from the wind, rain, or other weather conditions, but they were at the mercy of the temperature of the day. When I asked about this, the editor told me that there was some limited heat employed during the winter just to make it tolerable for the staff, although they all wore coats, caps and gloves during the winter months. She went on to explain that during the summer fans were used to keep the air moving, again for the comfort of the staff, but that it would be impractical to keep the entire warehouse at a constant temperature of, say, 72 degrees. Since then I haven't been too worried about the temperature of my books; I probably wouldn't put them up in the attic to be exposed to the extremes of summer, but I don't feel the need to keep them in the den where they can enjoy the same temperatures as my family.

Mice/Insects – These little beasties can be as devastating as a fire – it's one thing to find that a mouse has been nibbling on the corner of one of your book boxes, but quite another to discover that a swarm of paper-eating insects has infiltrated every single box and destroyed have of your books. Remember that warehouse I just talked about? I also noticed that they had a feline mascot with a plush bed up on a desk by the front door. The editor told me that they had visited a local animal shelter a few years ago and adopted a young cat. They made him feel welcome, fed him, gave him water and shelter, and basically let him know that the warehouse was his home. As such, he rid the place of rodents in very short order. The pet cat transitioned into an actual employee, albeit one that got a little extra attention from everyone. There are many types of critters that can harm your books, so preventing them from doing so is a *very* real consideration when choosing a place to store your books.

Odors – First of all, I'm not here to wave some anti-smoking banner, but I will never allow anyone to smoke around my books. Not only because of the added threat of fire, but also because paper absorbs odors like a sponge absorbs water. One example that always comes to mind is an instance when I ordered a piece of pottery from Ebay. I paid for the item when I won the auction, and a few days later a box showed up on my front porch. I brought it into the kitchen and placed it onto the island, then grabbed a knife and began to cut through the packing tape. When I opened the box, I had to take a step back – it *reeked* of cigarette smoke! When I moved the packing paper aside, my hands began to stink, and by the time I found the piece of pottery and removed it from the box, I was gagging. The box and packing went immediately into the outside trashcan, and I scrubbed the pottery in the sink several times. At that point, I knew that I would never allow anyone to smoke where I stored my books. No way would I want a bookstore to open a box from me and be hit with such an unpleasant experience. It might make them hesitant to put them on the shelves, much less out on tables where passersby could pick them up and leaf through them. This can happen with any significant odors, though – for example, one evening not long ago I showered, dressed and went with friends to a favorite barbecue restaurant. When

I got home about an hour later, I laid out my clothes to put them on the next morning – after all, I'd only worn them for an hour or so. The next day I noticed that they had the strong smell of barbecue smoke, to the point where there was no way that I could wear them out. Pay attention to odors where your books are stored – the paper can and will easily absorb the smells, and that is how your book will be represented.

Theft/Vandalism – Now, I'm not all that worried about a band of thieves plotting to steal my supply of books. There probably isn't a huge black market demand for them. What does concern me, though, is vandalism. It is a realistic concern that someone could break into the place where my books are stored, and finding nothing that he perceives of value, could take out the frustration on my books. Why do people do things like that? Well, if I knew the answer, I'd be speaking at a national symposium on psychology instead of helping people publish their own books. The fact is, though, that there are just some bad people in the world. I have a friend who has a wonderful garden, and in it he has a couple of gazing balls – those round, mirrored balls about a foot in diameter that rest on pedestals and provide a beautiful accent to all the flowers and plants. The gazing balls have to be replaces every year, because at some point a vandal will steal them and smash them somewhere around town. It's a terrible thing, but it has happened for years. I can imagine someone with low morals and standards deciding that it would be fun to throw my books at cars from an overpass, to start a bonfire with them, or some other heinous act that would be devastating to my inventory. As unlikely as it may seem, security for your books is something to consider.

Convenience of Location – It doesn't seem like a big deal, but it can become one with time. I know an author who found a friend's garage to store his books in; the only problem was that it was thirty minutes away from home. While the storage was free and relatively safe, it was a full hour trip just to go get a few books to ship. It would be one thing if he was going there to get five cases of books every day, but instead he was having to expend the time and gasoline to pick up a few. Things spiraled downhill from there – he started making only two trips a week, so there was an added juggling of paperwork to keep up with what had been ordered and what had been shipped. A closer location would have been much better in his particular situation.

All of the potential problems that I've mentioned are very real and should be taken into account when you are selecting a place to store your books. Like I said before, they are tangible assets, and should be treated as such. Protect them the same way that you would protect bundles of your money if you were having to store them yourself.

WRAPPING UP YOUR BOOK PUBLISHING

Are you feeling a little overwhelmed by everything that we've talked about in the printing chapter? Don't worry... you wouldn't be human if you didn't. Some of this is probably a little familiar, but much of it may be terribly intimidating. Don't worry, though – you're not alone. Thousands of authors have gone through the process of publishing their own book, and after you make your way through the first experience, you'll find that it becomes second nature to you.

If you find yourself lost in the design process, you can consult with the person editing your book, laying it out, or designing the cover to answer any questions that you may have. When it comes to printing, there will be a customer service person who will be happy to shepherd you through the process. Remember that old saying: "There are no stupid questions." Don't hesitate to ask whomever you need to get the information that you require. I distinctly remember having a lot of initial about what was meant by the term "pages" when asking for a book quote. Did they mean the physical pieces of paper that would be in the book, the count described by the highest page number, the total number of pages that can be read in the book, or some other mysterious quantity that I didn't understand. Of course, you learned the answer to that question earlier in this section, but at the time I was greatly confused. Worse than that, though, I was too embarrassed to ask the printer about it – I thought that they would consider me to be such an amateur that they wouldn't want to waste their time with me. I finally summoned the courage to call the printer's customer service person, and with a lot of hesitation I finally explained my confusion. Without hesitation she said, "Oh, we get that question all the time. Here's what you need to give us for page count..." I felt relieved, but also a little foolish to be afraid to ask such a question. From then on, I've been bold when asking even the most basic or trivial of questions – and I've always found that there's someone out there with the answer who's more than happy to help me.

All that said, at the end of the publication process you will have your book in your hand... but what comes next? Well, no one wants a garage stacked up with cases of books, so you're going to have to get out there and convince people to buy them. Does that sound intimidating? Don't worry – I've been with you through all of the process so far, and I'm certainly not going to abandon you now. Let's sell some books!

Section Four – Sell it!

GULP! NOW WHAT DO I DO?

What does that song from the Grateful Dead say… "What a long, strange trip it's been." Well, we started out with the process of creating the idea, then from there moved into actually writing the book, and once that was done, talked about the process of publishing it. I'll bet that the whole thing has seemed a little strange because we've covered ground that you'd probably never even thought of. But that's why you invited me on the journey – to give you a helping hand along the way, and shed some light on the unfamiliar topics that would spring up in your path. We're now at the end of the journey, and it's time to wrap things up with some ideals on selling your book. There is something that I have to mention, though; one of my favorite authors once said that "all endings are really beginnings, we just don't know it at the time." I think that's especially appropriate with your project, because once you're holding your new book, the journey is not over… it is simply getting started. Remember what I said in the last section: no one wants a garage stacked up with cases of books! Unless you can get out there and persuade people to buy them, that's exactly what you're going to end up with. I'm going to help you avoid that situation, though, so let's get started!

But We've Always Done It That Way…

Whenever I hear these words, my skin bristles up and I know that someone is being a slave to past procedures. If you'll forgive me using the cliché, I know that whoever used those words is thinking *inside the box*. Yeah, everyone is using that term to death these days, and it's even been morphed into a slogan for a Mexican fast-food chain that coined the term, "think outside the bun."

It's appropriate here, though, because this entire book has been about doing things outside of the norm, and being successful at it. I want you to take the same path in the selling of the book – first, however, let's take a peek back into the box, into the "old, normal" way of doing things, because I want you to understand what was once expected of authors.

In Days Of Old, When Knights Were Bold…

Okay, so it's not that far back, but after you've immersed yourself in the new world of publishing you may think that it was. The old publishing world is extremely different from what we've been talking about in this book. Let's break it down a little.

In the old days of publishing, after you've suffered through the process of submitting your book to publisher after publisher, a major house might finally purchase your book, print it, put it in their catalog, and hope that bookstores ordered it. The tasks of you, as an average author, would include setting up your own book signings, developing and producing a press kit, booking radio and television interviews, and getting any press that you can to review your book.

All that is terribly easy to say, but very tough to actually do. There have been scores of books written on the subject of promoting a book that has been traditionally published, and all those things that I just mentioned were the duties of the author. If you go down that path, you'll spend time calling bookstores to set up appearances, printing off press kits to send to the media in hopes of some publicity, setting up speaking engagements where you'll spend your own gas to drive and put on programs to promote your book, and generally just doing any and every kind of appearance that you can. Why? Well, there are two reasons: 1) you want your book to sell copies so that you'll make money through royalties, and 2) your publisher will judge you not only on book sales, but also on the amount of effort that you've put forth in promoting it.

Of course, when one of your book sells, the bookstore gets about half of the cover price. From what remains, the distributor gets a cut, the publisher gets a large piece, and if you have an agent he or she will get a percentage as well. Whatever crumbs that are left over will go to you, the author, and your part can be surprisingly small. I can't tell you how many first-time authors I know that have been crushed when they get that first royalty check and see how miniscule it can really be.

Don't get too depressed, though. As with all the other aspects of the publishing world that we've talked about so far, I have some words of comfort for you. The world is changing, and I can show you to take advantage of it.

The first thing that you might have already noticed is that whether you are promoting a book that came from a major publishing house, or one that you published on your own, you do the exact same of work to publicize it. You're going to expend the same amount of energy on the task; the only difference is that if it's your book instead of one belonging to a publishing house, you will make much, much more money... if you market it successfully, that is. So spend some time talking about that subject.

A Primer in Book Sales

Let's start with the basics – do you know the difference between marketing and sales? There is definitely a distinction between the two, and you need to clearly understand it. Think of it like this: marketing is what gets them to the table... sales is what closes the deal!

Marketing encompasses everything that you do to reach your prospects and persuade them that they need your product. In contrast, sales is everything that you do to close the deal and get the buyer to take out his wallet. Both marketing and sales are crucial to the success of your book; the two processes complement each other, and you must focus equally on both.

The marketing that you do consists of the techniques that you use to reach potential buyers; it is the message that prepares the buyer for the sale. Your marketing can consist of any number of techniques: paid advertising, web marketing, viral marketing, direct mail, book reviews, and other techniques you've probably heard of. Some can work extremely well, while others are a waste of time if not done correctly.

Sales usually involves interpersonal interaction. Whether you are doing a book signing at a store or manning your table at the back of the room after a speaking engagement, you will often need to personally communicate with the potential buyer. There are occasions, however, when you will rely on your written word to close the sale – situations like a sales letter or a web page. In one form or another, however, direct communication is crucial in the world of sales.

It is important to know which of the two functions – marketing or sales – that you are working with. If you're getting attention, driving traffic to a website, etc., that's marketing… you are driving customers to the table. If you're actually taking orders, receiving money, and closing deals… that's sales.

Another two concepts that are also related are features and benefits, and you must also be able to distinguish between them. Commonly accepted marketing wisdom says that, between those two, customers always prefer benefits. While features can be important, they take a back seat. When looking at your book, or any product for that matter, people want to know: *What's in it for me?*

Features may or may not provide benefits to a consumer. For example, if you are shopping for a home water heater, you will find that in general they are white in color. If you happened across one that was green, that would be a feature of that particular water heater. Does it add to your home water-heating experience? I seriously doubt it; because water heaters are usually hidden away from sight in a closet, the color isn't a positive or negative factor. On the other hand, if a water heater model has the latest technology (feature) and it can heat water five times faster than any other one on the market today at a fraction of the cost (benefit), then that is a feature/benefit that could be important to a consumer. Features are more or less "characteristics" of items. Benefits are the results you experience.

A Benefit is something good that gives value or pleasure. With the water heater that we just talked about, one "feature" is that it has the latest water-heating technology; the "benefit" is that you get hot water faster than anyone on your block. Benefits are always good, and they add something to your life.

In case the two concepts are still a little confusing, here's a chart that gives some good examples of features and benefits for items:

Item	Feature	Benefit
Air Conditioner	It comes with a programmable thermostat.	Your home will remain nice and cool during the summer.
Microwave Oven	Includes pre-programmed food settings.	Cooks foods conveniently and fast.
Hairspray	Made with eco-friendly ingredients.	Holds your hair in place throughout the day.
Web Design Service	HTML and Java programming, with keyword embedding.	You get a sleek, professional website.
Puppy	His bloodline goes back to several national champions.	Loves you unconditionally, and is delighted to see you come home every day.

When you're talking about your book, you have to be very clear as to what its features and benefits are. If you were to write a book on weight loss, here are some possible features of your book:

- It is 8.5" x 5.5" in size.
- It is ¾ inches thick.
- The printing is done on acid-free, permanent opaque pages.
- You lost weight last year, and put your techniques into the pages of the book.
- It has a black cover with bright white lettering for the title.
- It costs $18.95 retail.

Will any of those features make the consumer purchase the book? Well, probably not directly. The fact that it is the same size book that he's used to will lend a familiarity to the product. If it has a nice cover, that will give it eye appeal. Evidence that the author has some knowledge of the product gives it credibility. Still, no single one of those features alone will sell the book. On the other hand, if you can tell the consumer, "Read this book and you can lose ten pounds in thirty days!" that is a benefit that will catch their attention in our weight-obsessed culture.

Before we wrap up this primer in book sales section, there is one other concept to mention. We've talked about marketing versus sales, features versus benefits, but there is a physical, mechanical aspect of sales – the purchase process.

I know people who have put a ton of money into marketing their product, and then invested the time for its sales. They highlight and concentrate on the benefits. When it comes time for the customer to make the purchase, however, it is so complicated that it drives away the sale.

An example of a positive experience is Amazon.com – I've bought a lot of books from them, and my account is set up with something that they call "one click ordering." My shipping address, billing address, and credit card information is already in the system, when I'm shopping all I have to do is to log in when I first get to the website. From that point on anytime I want to purchase a book I just click on a single button, then confirm the order, and it is literally on the way to me. It's truly that easy, which is why I buy so much from that company. The best thing was that the account was pretty much automatically set up for me the first time that I shopped at Amazon.

Contrast that to a website I was on a few weeks ago. I'd done a web search for a book on a particular subject, and I ended up on the website of an author who had written a book that looked exactly like what I wanted. I enjoy buying directly from authors when I can, because I know that is beneficial for them, so I clicked on the order button and was taken directly to the shopping cart system for his site. I was expecting to put in my address, credit card, etc., but what I was surprised by was the complexity of the system. I still tried to use it, but finally abandoned it when I found out what all was expected of me. First of all, I had to set up a profile complete with test questions in case I forgot my password, every kind of information and demographic about me that you can imagine, and other items that I couldn't begin to see the relevance of. When I was finished, an email would be sent to me automatically that would contain my login and password.

At that point I would have to log back into the website and go back through the purchase procedure, this time while "logged in." Know what I did? I bailed on the author's website and purchased the book off Amazon with one click.

No matter how good your sales, marketing, features and benefits are, if you don't give the consumer a good ordering experience, you will miss sales. It's as simple as that.

Test Your Marketing/Sales Plan!

You'd be shocked to learn just how many people put together a marketing/sales plan for their book, launch it unceremoniously, and then sit back to see whether or not it succeeds. Such an approach drives me crazy! Unless you test and tweak any plan that you are thinking about implementing, you can waste time, money, and probably most importantly, sales leads.

When I think about testing, I think of how I used to get things from my mother. I'd throw out the request, "Ma, can I have a Popsicle?"

I'd gauge the response that she gave me, which was often, "No, it's too close to dinner!"

Since that didn't work, I'd test another approach. "Ma, it's really hot and I need to cool off." With this one, I was trying to play on her concern for my health.

Unfortunately, I'd often hear a reply that I still didn't like: "Then drink a glass of water."

Foiled again. Still, if I felt like there was a twist that I could put on the health aspect, I would certainly try it. "But Ma, water just isn't cold enough. It's not the same thing!"

In such an exchange, it sometimes seemed like she wasn't even listening; she'd simply kick back objections to any argument I tried. For example, she'd probably respond with, "Look, just drink a glass of water and sit down in the shade for a while."

That's the point where I'd have to get a little creative. Since my health and comfort angle wasn't working, I'd switch gears and look for some incentive – something that I could offer her. For example, I might come back with, "But, Ma, I want to carry out the trash, but I need to cool off first."

After a heavy sigh, she would acquiesce and respond with something such as, "Okay, carry out the trash and then I'll give you a Popsicle."

I really wanted the Popsicle, but the trick was presenting the request to my mother in such a way that would entice her to give me one. I kept testing my marketing message until I was successful and there was an ice-cold, delicious Popsicle in my hand.

Testing your marketing message is crucial. It's not just about making a sale, but instead getting the most sales at the highest profit – and that comes from testing. Also, if your test can't prove a profit, then you know not to proceed with the campaign.

As an example, in Direct Marketing we used to mail sales letters to mailing lists of hundreds of thousands of names. These lists were carefully selected to contain names of people with a proven interest in our product. But before we mailed the whole list, we'd refine our sales letter by doing some simple testing.

First we'd test the headline by sending our letter to the first thousand names on the list and gauging the response that we received. Then, we'd change the headline to something we thought might be more powerful, and measure that response against the first letter. If the response improved, that letter would be the 'control' until another one could prove to beat its results.

We'd test everything about the campaign, though: the headline, the sub-head, the body copy, the guarantee, and the price. We'd continue testing until we believed that we had the best letter, and it proved itself to be profitable. At that point we'd mail the whole list.

The next logical question is how we knew that the letter was profitable. The answer is pure and simple math. For example, if we mailed 1,000 letters and got 20 orders (2% – pretty much an industry standard) and our price point was $49, the gross sales were $980. It cost us, at the time, about .67 to mail a letter including the printing, envelope, postage, and the name, so our cost was $670 – keep in mind that we had to pay for the entire mailout of 1,000 letters, even though we only got 20 orders. We would therefore have a gross profit of $310. Not a rousing success, but if we could make $310 per 1,000 names and our list had 500,000 entries, we could gross $155,000 with the mail campaign.

Of course, we were constantly trying to improve the results, and we did that by testing and monitoring the results. Any change that was made to the letter that improved our results meant an automatic increase in sales and profits.

The same thing holds true in other forms of marketing messages whether it's email, print ads, radio or whatever medium you choose to work in. It is always necessary – no, it is downright crucial – to test your marketing/sales message before you commit to the entire campaign.

In the world of email, we test similar things: the subject line, the open rate (the percentage of people actually opening the email to read it) and the click-through rate (the percentage of people who clicked on the advertising link in the email to learn more. If I had a large list of 'juicy' email addresses I'd begin my campaign by testing these statistics. By using a basic mailing list program, I can find out how many of the emails were actually opened by the recipient – which tells me how my subject line is working. You probably know what I'm talking about, since you probably get emails every day that you either click on to read, or immediately send to the trash.

Of those that opened the email, I would then look at how many of the recipients read the email and clicked on the 'live link' that took them to my sales page or an order page. Each of these items is useful information: whether the recipient immediately deleted the message, read it and took no action, read it and clicked on the sales link, or ended up buying the product.

I would send a few thousand emails at a time and take a look at the results. That would tell me what needed to be tweaked, as shown in this chart:

Result	Correction Needed
People aren't opening the email	Subject line needs modification
Recipients open the email, but aren't clicking on the link	The email sales letter needs enhancing
Recipients open the email, click on the link, but don't buy the product	The website sales letter and/or price needs tweaking

Print advertising works much the same way: placing an ad in a newspaper, and then testing the results. I'd choose one newspaper, for example, and then run the advertisement that I'd created. If the results didn't measure up I would make modifications to it: first the heading, then the text, etc. When I finally had the perfect ad, I would then run it in all of the papers – sometimes thousands of different newspapers across the country.

A similar process is true for magazine ads, except that the lead time can be much longer. It can sometimes take up to two months to get your ad placed, and so the whole testing process is much slower. To keep from wasting a lot of time, I would first test an advertisement in a newspaper first, refine it as many times as needed to make it successful, and then move it to a magazine.

I have to stress, thought, that all marketing that I've done is what is called 'Direct Response' – which means that an immediate, measurable result is expected – which is what makes it measurable and testable. This is as compared to some advertising agency antics that don't expect feedback or results – having something that you can actually measure is extremely important.

In other words, my sales letter will ask for an order... and that gives me the ability to measure its effectiveness. We often use two-step ads that have a phone number to call for more information or a free report so that we can measure results. Statistically, 87% of responders to a two-step ad will eventually buy. The bottom line is that without a measurable response, you're simply not able to test.

As you can see, proper scientific testing and measuring of your sales message is crucial to your success. The amount of time and research that you put into testing your ad can make you a rich man, or at least, keep you from becoming a poor one!

How Will You Collect The Money?

We've spent some time talking about how to market and sell your product – it's time to take a break from that and look at how you're actually going to collect payment when someone orders your book. While there are many companies out there that will process orders for you, we're going to look at the main two options: your own merchant account, and PayPal. Before proceeding, let me be honest with you; the world of online payment acceptance varies widely, and no matter what statements I make, someone could certainly find exceptions. What I am going to talk about in this section is a general discussion of your two main options.

The things that I'm saying are only guidelines for you to consider when choosing your own particular method of collecting money.

The first thing that I want to talk about is a classic merchant account. Basically, this is a partnership between you and a bank; a line of credit is extended to you for the purpose of accepting credit cards. There is usually a monthly fee for the service no matter how much (or little) you sell, and then on top of that there is a per-transaction charge. Depending on your account, you may have to establish different relationships with different credit card companies: American Express, Visa, Master Card, Discover, etc.

If you are selling enough quantity that covers the monthly fee, the per-transaction charge is small enough to make this an attractive option.

Merchant accounts aren't without their problems, though. Many require a long-term contract ranging from one to five years; should you need to exit the relationship with the merchant account there is often an early termination fee, and if a time comes when you can't pay the monthly fee or the early termination fee, your credit can be affected.

Those problems aren't common, however. When you pay for a product or service with a credit card that is scanned when you check out, it is being run though a merchant account. There are literally millions of individual accounts like this across the nation and for the most part, they all run smoothly.

Let's contrast that with PayPal. Unless you've been living in a cave in the Himalayas for the last ten years, you've probably already heard of the PayPal service. In fact, I'd be in shock if most of the people reading this book didn't already have an account set up.

For those who may not be familiar with it, though, the company was formed in 1998 for the purpose of making simple monetary transactions from one person to another over the web. Just a couple of years later, people using the online auction site Ebay noticed it, and PayPal soon became the preferred method of payment. The two services seemed to fit so well together that in 2002 Ebay purchased PayPal for $1.5 billion dollars.

Since that time it has grown to be one of the largest online payment systems around, serving some fifty countries and sixty million customers. Over fifty million dollars a day is transacted by people using PayPal – and there are many, many banks that don't see that kind of business. It's collected many awards over the years: the *People's Voice Award for Best Finance Site*, One of the *Top 100 Websites by PC Magazine*, One of the *Top 25 Companies by Fortune Small Business*, and *Forbes' Favorite Email Payment Processor*, to name but a few. I'd be remiss if I didn't also mention that they've also picked up their share of criticism – there are entire websites dedicated to people who feel like they have been wronged by PayPal… and believe me, there are some very real horror stories. All-in-all, though, by an order of magnitude there are many more people who love PayPal than those who don't like it. I think of it like the world-famous hamburger chain McDonald's. There are millions of people who love their food and eat there on a regular basis. Still, you'll occasionally find a person who got really, really bad service on a visit and has launched a personal campaign against the fast-food giant. You'll find similar circumstances with PayPal.

If there is any weak point about PayPal, it is that it was originally designed to be a simple way for one person to send money to another over the web, something that made it perfect for Ebay customers. Now that it has become so popular, the company has made a conscious effort to evolve into a full-blown shopping cart system... but not without its growing pains. For a long time it was like trying to fit the proverbial round peg into the square hole. As the months go by, however, PayPal is becoming more and more sophisticated.

In comparing the two, there are pros and cons for each. And, you may already have a merchant account that you're using, or you may be very proficient with PayPal. The only other point that I'd make at this point is that it costs nothing to get set up with PayPal, and you can use it to get started until your sales reach a point where a Merchant Account is warranted.

Whether you decide to use a Merchant Account or PayPal, there are some industry terms that you should be familiar with. I want to go ahead and present them so that as you explore your options, you will understand the language that is being spoken.

Automated Clearing House (ACH): A credit card processing service that is networked with other such services to exchange and handle electronic debit/credit transactions.

Address Verification Service (AVS): A mechanism used for verifying that the address provided by a customer using a credit card matches the address on record for the cardholder at the issuing bank.

Annual Fee: A fee charged to merchants to use the service

Application Fee: This is the initial fee for processing the information necessary to set up an account.

Authorization: The process whereby a transaction is approved by an issuing bank, authorized agent, or Visa/ MasterCard on behalf of that issuer, before the transaction is completed by the merchant via telephone or terminal.

Card Present: A term that describes a transaction when the customer is personally using his or her credit card and the vendor is able to actually touch the card. For example, a card-present transaction would be when a card holder pays a restaurant bill with his card by giving it to the server. A non-card-present transaction would be if someone purchased something over the internet.

Chargeback: A chargeback occurs when a cardholder disputes a charge on his bill. When that happens, the amount in dispute is immediately deducted from the merchant's account, and a dispute resolution process is started.

CVV2: This is also known as the "security code," the "secret code," or any number of other terms. What it is, though, is the three-digit security code printed on the back of most credit cards in the signature block. The CVV2 program was implemented for fraud prevention, the thinking being that if you had to flip the card over and read a number of the back, a buyer had the actual card and not just an imprint of the front.

Discount Rate: This is the fee taken by the bank as a percentage of all sales transactions. For example, if the discount rate happens to be 1.50%, then the discount rate fee is $1.50 for a $100.00 charge.

Doing Business As (or simply DBA): The DBA is the name the public sees, even though it might not be the name that the bank and the IRS knows you by. If you had three websites called babyclothes.com, mamaclothes.com, and daddyclothes.com, all of which you conducted business in under your own name, you would still probably need to file a DBA for each one so that you can receive payments, write off expenses, etc.

eCommerce: This term has slowly encroached its way into our vocabulary, and simply refers to business done over the internet and/or processed electronically.

Gateway: In the world of merchant accounts, a gateway is a service which connects the shopping cart with the credit card processor. Basically, the gateway accepts the data in the shopping cart's format, translates it to the credit card processor's format and then transmits it to the card processor.

It then does approximately the same thing in reverse to return the authorization and other codes to the shopping cart program.

Gateway fee: The monetary fee for using the services of a gateway system (as described above).

Guarantor: Since merchant accounts are personally guaranteed, a guarantor is the company or person who agrees to guarantee any processing losses that the merchant bank incurs. For example, if you are opening your business babyclothes. com, you may be required to personally be the guarantor for the business. If there's ever a problem, the company comes after your personal assets, not the company's.

Imprinter: Otherwise known as the "knuckle-buster," this now old-fashioned, manual, slide device was used to produce an image of the raised (embossed) characters on a credit card on a transaction slip. If you have one of these, please donate it to your local museum.

Internet Merchant Account: This is a hybrid of the standard merchant account, and it represents a relationship between a retailer and a merchant bank that is specifically in place to allow the retailer to accept credit card payments from customers over the Internet.

Issuing Bank: Quite simply, the bank that issues a credit card.

Keyed Transaction: A keyed transaction is one where the information from a credit card is manually entered into a terminal or computer. A transaction is keyed because either the credit card is not present at the time the transaction is entered, or the equipment being used to process the transaction can't read the card. This happened to me a while back when a card that I had been carrying in my wallet for a while developed a bad magnetic strip.

Monthly Minimum: The minimum amount of discount fees charged by a merchant account provider in a given month. If you don't have that much in sales, then you are expected to make up the difference out of your own pocket.

Monthly Volume: The maximum monthly dollar amount that a merchant is approved to process in credit card transactions. The MV is important for underwriter consideration of the file and also helps to determine what type of documentation will be required with the file.

Point of Sale (POS): This is just the physical location where a credit card sale is completed.

Reserve: Some merchant account companies will hold back a percentage of your sales to cover disputes and chargebacks. While it protects them against losses, the credit card companies get to draw interest off the reserve money while it is waiting to be paid to you. Believe it or not, this can be a major source of income for credit card companies.

Secure Server: A must for doing business on the web; such a service encrypts credit card information that is passed between the individual sitting at a computer and the server that is processing his credit card. This encryption protects the user's credit card information, and is expected in today's world when doing business on the web.

Shopping Cart: An automated system that allows you to purchase multiple products while browsing through a website. If you've every purchased products through Amazon.com, you've seen a classic example of a shopping cart.

Statement Fee: A terrible little fee (except for the credit card companies, for whom it benefits) that is charged to produce your merchant account statement each month and mail it to you. This is something that your electric company, phone company, and gas company does for free every month, by the way.

Swipe: One of my favorite terms, since when I grew up, this term meant, "to steal." In the world of credit card processing, though, this term means to physically slide a credit card through a reader. For anyone who has ever purchased anything at Wal-Mart, when they slide your card through their machine at the checkout, they are swiping it.

Transaction Fee: A fee charged to you as the merchant any time that you process a credit card purchase.

Voice/VRU: This is an automated Voice Response Transaction, typically used for authorizing a credit card charge over the telephone.

I know that all these terms may not make complete sense at the moment, but when you start delving into the business of accepting credit cards, you will find the knowledge of them indispensible.

Inbound Telemarketing And Telephone Sales

I had a conversation with a friend of mine who was selling a product with orders to be taken by phone. He hired a person to receive the inbound calls, and to fill the orders for shipping when the phone wasn't ringing. A desk was purchased, a phone line was installed, and everything was set and ready to go. The product was advertised in a magazine, and the day that it hit the stands, his new employee sat there poised to pick up the telephone… but the phone was silent. As the next week went by, there were still no calls. By the third or fourth week, it was obvious that the ad wasn't working. All of the expense had been a complete loss at that point.

On the other hand, I heard story at a conference about another entrepreneur who decided to handle his phone orders himself, and he ended up losing many, many potential orders because he'd done such a good job with ad composition and placement that the phone was ringing off the wall. He simply couldn't handle it himself, and ended up losing orders and creating a lot of ill will when people couldn't get through.

So what is the answer? Well, you've heard me say it before: test your campaign. Be ready for a large-scale response, but as much as I hate to say it, also be prepared for a total shut-out. Not that you don't have a good product, but marketing a product is a continual exercise in trial and error.

You may want to initially handle the orders yourself, but I'd recommend locating a call center that you can quickly transition over to should the need arise. A call center is a business set up with lots of phones & order-taking professionals who can handle everything for you in a turn-key fashion.

There are mechanical things to consider – for example, how do they pick up your phone number? You may have been lucky and scored the number 1-800-MY-PRODUCT, but they will have to be able to answer it if they take over your call center traffic.

Believe me, they've addressed all the issues that you can imagine, and you just need to make sure that you have all your ducks in a row should you need to turn to the call center option. As I said before, you can field your own calls until they get overwhelming, and then make a seamless switch over to a call center should the need arise.

Fulfillment Options

Once someone has purchased your product, the order must be fulfilled. That presents yet another quandary. If you are getting fifty book orders a day, then you may be spending most of your time printing labels, stuffing books into padded envelopes, sticking on postage, etc.

On the other hand, if you are getting five orders a day it wouldn't make sense for you to hire someone else to do the job.

There are businesses that do nothing but fulfillment, but my basic message here is to simply do the math. As with using a call center, it only makes sense if the traffic warrants it.

Let's run a few numbers. Assume that you have a book that sells for $20.00 (I love round numbers for examples), and it costs you $4.00 per book. If postage is $2.00 per book, and a padded mailing envelope is another dollar, then for every web order that you fulfill personally you'll make $20 minus the $5 book cost, $2 shipping, and $1 envelope... or $12 profit for every book that you sell and ship yourself.

Now assume that you engage a fulfillment service that takes 60% of the sale price for taking the order, packing the book, then shipping it. That means you will only get $8 profit for every book ordered.

Does it make sense to use the service? Well, if you're getting two dozen orders a day, it may be worth the $4 per book sacrifice. On the other hand, if you are only receiving three or four calls a day then it is worth your time to handle it yourself.

So what is the moral of this story? Like I've said, test your marketing plan. Get ready for the overflowing success, but be prepared for a setback that requires a few tweaks.

A lot of that goes back to the next topic that we'll be exploring... knowing your market before you wade into it.

KNOW YOUR MARKET AND HOW TO FIND THEM

If I could put a flag on the most important section of this book, this would be it. If you write the most informative, well-crafted book in the history of mankind, but don't know where you're going to sell it, it's like practicing archery while blindfolded – you'll never hit the target. Unless you keep your eye keenly on the specific target, in this case your market, your books will sit in boxes stacked in your garage.

Believe me, I've seen books that were total train-wrecks that sold like hotcakes, all because the author knew his or her market. I won't directly criticize any author, but there is one person that is a household name whose book was a national sensation. I bought it for that reason, and read it… and kept asking "Why?" It was badly constructed and written even worse. The bottom line, though, was that he had a plan to visit a particular type of mom and pop bookstores across the country to market it, and slowly began to develop a following.

That book became a bestseller across the country, but he started it all with a grass-roots effort because he believed that he knew his audience… and he did. What I learned from him is that you have to know your market intimately – what they read, the websites that they visit, discussion groups that they frequent, etc.

Whenever someone tells me that they are writing a book, the first thing that I ask them is where they are planning to market it. In the world today, you must know exactly what your audience is, and how you are going to reach them. This section will explore different aspects of this crucial aspect of marketing your book.

Niche markets

There are barrels of money to be made in niche markets, yet a lot of entrepreneurs ignore them. They can be much easier to market into, and you can see incredible results.

So what are niche markets? Simply stated, they are an extremely focused part of the entire market. To target a product into a niche market, you need only find an area where a need exists and provide an acceptable solution. We've already talked about many niche markets: a book by an auto mechanic, a book on how to build a greenhouse, etc.

Let's look at the greenhouse book again. If you were to put it in a classic bookstore, you might sell one occasionally. On the other hand, if you could get it into the lawn and garden section of a hardware store, you might do quite well. Just imagine, though, if you could get a small booth at a lawn and garden show, and perhaps set up a small greenhouse behind your table as part of your display – I bet that you'd sell more at that one show than you would in a full year at a classic bookstore.

There are other things that you can do, however. You could take out an ad in a gardening magazine, or buy advertising space on a gardening website or blog. With niche markets the possibilities are endless. It's all about finding the niche and exploiting the opportunities.

How do I find Niche Markets?

If you've written a book on a particular subject, then chances are you already have an idea what some of the niche markets for it could be. I'd bet that as we've been talking about niche markets the wheels in your head were already starting to turn. Here are a few more just to add into the mix, though.

Highly targeted mailing lists can be purchased from companies such as infousa.com if you want to make direct mail one of your marketing campaigns. While services like this have been available for years, in today's information age they have become even more specific.

You can also find websites, blogs, and forums for your subject matter – in many cases you can join the discussion, and we'll talk about how to do that in the internet marketing section coming up.

The internet is a wonderful tool for uncovering niche markets. Web searches using a service such as Google can yield all sorts of ideas. For the greenhouse book example that we've been using, I would do a search for something like "home and garden trade shows" if I wanted to locate places for booth sales. On the other hand, if I wanted to book speaking engagements where I could sell the book at the back of the room, I'd simply search for something like "garden clubs." The possibilities are truly endless.

Finally, when looking for niche markets, think back to your own experiences. A friend of mine has a perfect niche market, and he does well with it. He is a writer by trade, and has done both national and regional books in his career. While on vacation one day he popped into a local bookstore in a town whose main industry is tourism. He was looking for a book about the city and its history, but soon discovered that one didn't exist. A light bulb went off instantly in his mind, and he immediately went into research mode to gather all the information that he could about the city on that trip. Several months, many phone calls, and at least a return trip or two later, he had a book on the city that he placed into the local stores. Because tourism is the main industry there, and tourists love to buy books, my friend does better with that one, focused book than he does with his national titles. He has a perfect niche market for his book… and you could probably think of some for your book based on your own experiences.

Your Average Customer Profile

The final thing that I want to mention before moving into a discussion about selling is that it is very important to know your audience – and to do that, sit down and write a profile of who your average customer would be.

If your book is about military history, statistics show that your average customer will be male. On the other hand, if you've written about quilting, a woman will usually purchase your book.

Is that person young, middle-aged, or senior? What race is he or she? Is national heritage a contributing factor? All of these things make a difference, and can help you not only identify a niche, but can help you design your marketing plan.

The following list includes these factors, as well as some others that you may not have thought of. Some will matter in your case, others won't, but you can use them as a springboard to putting together your average customer profile:
- Gender
- Age
- Race

- National Heritage
- Education Level
- Occupation
- Marital Status
- Family Size
- Religion
- Geographic Location
- Political Affiliation
- Armed Forces Service
- Hobbies
- Economic Class

You can probably think of more, and as I said, all won't apply to your particular case. Still, it is crucial that you get a clear understanding of whom the person is that you'll be targeting with your marketing efforts. Sit down and write out the specific items that make up the profile. Once that is done, you'll be surprised how much it helps with your marketing.

KNOW HOW TO SELL INTO YOUR MARKET

Once you have identified your market, it is extremely important to have a plan ready to get your sales message in front of the prospective buyers. As it turns out, you have many options at your fingertips: traditional direct marketing, in-person appearances such as speeches or book signings, internet marketing, or integrated marketing, which are just combinations of all of those. We're going to wrap up this marketing section by taking an in-depth look at all of these different ways that you can get books in front of people and entice them to buy.

Traditional Direct Marketing

Traditional direct marketing has been around for years in the form of direct mail, print ads, and infomercials. I should ad that not only has it simply been around, but it has been used successfully by many people. You may remember that we touched on the subject back in the "Testing Your Market/ Sales Plan" section of this book, but it bears mentioning in a little more detail here.

Direct mail continues to be a cornerstone of traditional direct marketing – I am reminded of this fact every time I check my mailbox. I don't know how many mailing lists I've been added to over the years, but the number must be huge. My mailman tells me that I get more mail than everyone else on the block combined, and there isn't a day that goes by that he doesn't stop out in front of my house. A lot of people send me a lot of direct make solicitations.

One thing to keep in mind about direct mail is that an average return is 2%. That is to say, for every 100 pieces of direct mail that you send out, two people will buy your product... in this case, your book. Using some of the same figures that we've kicked around before, let's say that you see $12.00 profit on a book sold directly to a customer, and that it costs $.67 for every piece of mail (postage, paper, printing, envelope, etc.). If you send out those 100 sales letters you'll spend $67.00 to make $24.00 – not a good return on your investment.

On the other hand, sending out 1000 sales letters would cost you $670.00, and would net you $240.00... still not worth the effort. And if you send out 10,000 sales letters the up-front investment would be $6,700.00, but the return would be only $2400.00. Are you seeing a pattern? Good, because this is extremely important to keep in mind: to merely break even, your profit margin on 2% return must always equal the cost of the entire mailing.

As you may have surmised, this model isn't optimal for just a single book unless the profit on the book is high, or the production cost of the mailing is significantly lower. In our example, the book profit would have to be $35.00 for the concept to work – and that's just a little above break-even. If you can bundle your products, say, offer the book, a related video, and an audio presentation, the profit can be taken up to a range that is much more attractive.

There is another factor that is as important as the cost, and that is the mailing list. Consider the following items:
1. You can purchase a mailing list of 10,000 names.
2. But, you can also be assured that the list contains names and addresses that have been validated within the last six months.
3. Finally, you know that everyone on the list fits within the demographics of your average customer profile.

Notice that with each step the mailing list becomes more and more valuable to you. An inexpensive list of 10,000 names isn't any good to you if half of the letters will be returned to you. It also isn't that helpful if you can only hope that the people on the list are interested in your product – you're leaving your success to a random factor. Thankfully, mailing lists are available that are highly targeted in nature, and it can certainly increase your results. By doing a simple web search, you can find many sources that sell mailing lists with many beneficial attributes.

There have been volumes written on the subject of direct mail marketing, and if you want to use it in your campaign, you will even be able to find a lot of information online. It's not a hard process, but it can be expensive… so remember to test your plan as you go!

The other aspect of traditional direct marketing to mention here are print ads in newspapers and magazines. They aren't as much work with the printing, stuffing envelopes, and stamping of direct mail, but after that point, they become very similar. You must compose the ad in the same way that you do the sales letter; you test the ad in a limited way, and then gage the results.

One aspect of print ads that can work to your advantage is classified ads. They can be inexpensive, and based on the periodical that you choose, very focused on your target. Classified ads give you the ability to continue tweaking the text of the advertisement until you see results that meet your expectations. At that point, you can either expand your classified ad to other publications, or use the ad as a basis for a larger print ad to run in magazines or other periodicals.

Traditional direct marketing is comprised of tried and true methods that you should not ignore. In today's online electronic world, though, there are other options to consider – those of internet marketing.

INTERNET MARKETING

This ever-evolving marketing opportunity can be a little intimidating. After all, I know people who are literally marketing geniuses who have made their money by the old tried-and-true direct mail marketing. They know everything in the world about that business and have honed their skills to perfection over the years... but they can barely turn a computer on and read their email, much less construct a web page to sell their product. If you find such a person and explain the mere basics of the internet, in the process you will notice that person's eyes glaze over as they stop paying attention.

The problem that I find with many people is that they're cyberphobic – they have some built-in, deep-seated fear of the internet. This isn't a new concept, or even something unique to computers, though You see, I have a friend who has the thing with automobile repair. He is extremely computer-savvy, has a degree in Computer Science from one of the top engineering schools in the nation, yet he's told me on several occasions that he could never, ever be a mechanic. He doesn't understand how cars work, and even with all his learning he truly believes that the subject is far beyond his capability.

That's why I always stress that the world of the internet isn't as complex as you think. There are five-year-old kids that send emails every day, and ninety-year-old seniors who have their own website. When it comes to the internet, you are truly limited by what you believe that you can achieve... and believe me, you can achieve a lot.

Although it is getting a little crowded, the world wide web is a place that is perfect for an entrepreneur to do marketing. You can launch your marketing campaign for little or no money, because there are no costs that are associated with classic direct marketing – no printing, envelopes, postage, etc. In fact, I once heard the marketing giant Tom Antion say, "I love the internet; it costs nothing to fail there!" I thought that was a profound quote. What he is actually saying is that you can test your ideas without a lot of initial investment, and if they don't work, you can simply tweak the campaign and try again with no substantial monetary outlay. It's a place that is perfect for people like you and me.

Websites

No matter what your overall marketing plans are for your book, in today's day and age you're going to need a website. You can pay to have one constructed for you if you wish, and you'll probably get one that is very professional. Be aware, though, that people who don't know how to construct a website can find themselves at the mercy of those who do. You can get a site for $100, or for $5000 – it depends on what you're willing to spend.

I don't want to give any hard advise at this point, because I've seen elaborate websites that bring in thousands of dollars every month, but I've seen simple, straightforward sites that do the same thing. Like everything in marketing, it all comes down to your product, your presentation, and the audience that you've gathered.

Remember Antion's saying about the internet, though – it doesn't cost anything to fail there. If you want to save money, test your idea by setting up your own site and tweaking it to gage sales. You'd be surprised how easy that process really is. It's outside the scope of this book to explain basic website construction, though; besides, it's been done over and over again by other authors. If you'd like to try it yourself, just visit the local bookstore and you will find volume after volume on the subject of basic website design.

You can process the transactions using PayPal or a similar company and then fulfill your own orders. And while I don't want to completely talk you out of having someone else design your site, doing it yourself is a way to learn and master the web. As you're thinking about doing that, here are a few other things to keep in mind:

- Make sure that you're clear about the purpose of your website – to sell your book. Your sell-site is not the place to post vacation photos (unless your book is about travel), discuss football scores (unless it's a book about fantasy football), or provide recipes (unless... well, you get the picture). Keep your focus on the website and the reason that you have it.
- Decide whether you're going to do the site yourself, or contract it out. I talked about that a page or so ago, and either can work out well. Another alternative is to get a friend who can help you get started in the process – kind of like a mentor.
- Map out how your site is going to flow – draw it out, in fact. You'll probably have a top page that is either a stand-alone sell page, or an informational page that links down to the sub-pages that provide more information – including a sell page.

- Decide how people will navigate through your website. Will you have navigation buttons down the left side of the page? Across the top? You've no doubt seen many examples of website navigation techniques, and they are all appropriate on the proper site. As you think about your website, determine the best way for visitors to navigate through it.
- Think about your website's appearance and your brand. No matter how or where someone lands on one of your pages, it needs to establish the look and feel that you want related to your product. No matter which of your website pages a visitor sees first, their experience needs to set the theme for your website as whole.
- You need to be aware of search engines when you're designing your website, and that's a topic that deserves more than a few words. We'll talk about it more in the next section.
- "Content is King" – remember those words. No matter if you're simply posting a sell site on the web, or a multi-page website, you need to do more than push your product. You need to have information about the subject and product that will attract visitors. If you are searching the web for a particular topic and stumble onto a particular site, if you immediately see that all it is doing is pushing a product, you may immediately surf away. On the other hand, if it gives you information and entices you to read further, and then provides you with an opportunity to buy a product with even more info, then it's a win/win for everyone. You get the information that you need, and the author makes a sale… all because of content.
- Allow visitor discussion and feedback. In today's world this is called "Social Media Marketing," which we

discuss in a separate chapter. You need to allow for this on your website, though, and one of the easiest forms is that of a blog. **www.blogger.com** allows you to set up and maintain a blog which will allow you to interact with your visitors, answering questions, addressing comments, but most of all, holding their interest in your topic.

- This is the most important thing that I'm going to say on the topic: CONTINUALLY TEST AND UPDATE YOUR WEBSITE! If it is not producing sales, find out why. Most web hosting services have statistics, and you can see how many people are coming to the site. If the number is low, then you need to start a campaign to drive traffic there. If there are many visitors but no sales, then your site needs adjusting. It is imperative that you are always looking for ways to increase sales on your website.

Those are just a few points to consider, but I hope that they help. Maintaining a website can be a tricky thing, but can pay huge dividends in the long run.

Ah Yes, Search Engines

After the last section you probably have a website planned for promoting your book – and you'll definitely need one. Keep in mind, though, that a website by itself a useless tool. Remember that old question, "If a tree falls in the forest and there's no one there to hear it, does it make a sound?" Well, I can't answer that one, but on the internet one might ponder a similar question: If a site is put on the 'net, and no one goes to visit it, does it really exist?

Just like the sounds of the tree that no one hears, if no eyes see your website, then it might as well not be there. If no one can find the website, then you won't sell a book – it's up to you to drive traffic to the site… hopefully in great numbers.

One of the best and most important ways to do this is by utilizing search engines. That said, let me be quick to say that it's impossible to say exactly how search engine algorithms work – they're carefully guarded secrets. Just like McDonald's guards its Secret Sauce recipe and Coca-Cola keeps its formula confidential, giants like Google won't give the slightest hint about how their search engine works. More than that, though, they are constantly tweaking it to make it yield better content results for the uses, and prevent webmasters from using tricks to drive traffic to their site.

Before we talk about ways to optimize your site for search engine placement, let me first give you a few warnings about things that can send your placement to the bottom of the search engine list, or get it downright banned. There are all sorts of supposed tricks and tips to help your site with search engines, but they can often hurt you instead.

For example, in the early days of the web some of the search engines used very rudimentary formulas such as how many times a topic was mentioned on a site. This led some webmasters to use a solid color background, and then make a list of a single word (the theme of the website – the term that they wanted the search engine to pick up) over and over again in the same color font as the background. If it was a site selling farm machinery, the web designer might use a green background, and then the word "tractor" in green a thousand times after the basic site content. When a human looked at the site, it just appeared that there was some extra green space at the bottom, but when a search engine program viewed the site electronically, it would record that the site had a thousand occurrences of the word "tractor," and it must be a site very relevant to that term.

Later, HTML (the language that web pages are written in) adopted keywords that were used to instruct web browsers regarding the site. These keywords were called "meta-tags," but this was also instantly abused. Porn sites would put all manner of terms in their meta-tag for site content: "apple, bear, century, driving, elephant, etc.," none of which had anything to do with the site, but they were trying to snag hits when anyone searched for one of those terms. It got so out of hand so quickly that the content keyword meta-tags are now ignored by search engines.

Both of the above techniques are known as "keyword stuffing" or "spamdexing," and if a search engine detects it in a website, that site will be given very low ranking or even dropped from search engine results.

There are several other deceptive techniques that have been used to try to deceive search engines:

Cloaking – a more sophisticated deception that is used by some webmaster, where the website delivers one page to search engines for indexing, while actually showing visitors a completely different page. This technique is also called "stealthing," and only web-savvy people know how to implement it. Even with all that work, though, it usually backfires – search engines such as Lycos, Hotbot and Excite have publically stated that they have taken steps to detect cloaked websites, and ban them from their index and result lists.

Doorway pages – these pages are set up for the sole purpose of causing a search engine to index the page a certain way for a certain keyword or theme. When the engine presents the link as part of a search result and the user clicks on it, they are immediately taken to a completely different site. Web designers using this technique sometimes copy the main page of popular web sites, and add code to immediately take the user to the real destination (e.g., a porn site).

Link farms – at one time search engines gave high marks to web pages with lots of links. Webmasters immediately jumped on this, creating groups of sites that link to other sites for the sole purpose of increasing their search engine ranking. Unlike perfectly valid links to sites with related information, sites that participate in link farming contain links to totally unrelated sites, a practice that is also called "link stuffing." Search engines such as Google hate link farms, and labels the that links they generate as spam. In fact, Google detests such sites so much that they may be completely removed from the search engine index if they're affiliated with link farms. This has frightened some webmasters, who have trimmed down or downright removed all outbound links from their sites.

Those are just a few of the clandestine techniques used by webmasters to improve their search engine ranking – some are simply trying to trick the search engines, while others such as porn sites are being maliciously deceptive. It's like playing blackjack at a Vegas casino, though. The house is genuinely happy to see you play honestly and win, but if you try to cheat, the consequences can be very bad.

The algorithms used by search engines have really become a science, and so the theories and speculations about how they work are far beyond the scope of this book. But you should be aware of the basics, and then pursue the details further as your project dictates.

If you were to do a search on Google for a particular term, you would be presented with a large number of 'hits,' or website links, containing information related to the term that you searched for. In other words, if you searched for the term 'greenhouses,' you would get back about ten million 'hits' and you would then have to start at page one and keep checking, reading, and visiting these sites until you found the information you specifically wanted.

If you wanted to refine your search to something more specific, you could use a set of keywords or a phrase such as, "types of glass used in greenhouses." The results are filtered for this specific query, and you would receive only about 300,000 'hits' and they will be specific to glass used in greenhouses.

Such a specific query can save the searcher tons of time and get them to what they want much quicker than a generic search.

If you happen to be in the greenhouse business and have information relevant to glass used in greenhouses, your website would probably be picked up in the search. Of course, it might be in the first position, or down at number 300,000, all depending on how the search engine has evaluated your site.

I find that when I do a web search, I usually only go through about the first five pages of results before I either find what I want or get bored with the whole thing. If you are indexed far down into the field, chances are that I'm never going to see your site.

The way that search engines create this index are by using programs that automatically traverse the web and gather information about web sites. These programs are called 'spiders.' If you have a good site with relevant and useful information, your site will get a higher rating by the spider and it appear closer to the top of the search. If you have a junk site that is mostly commercial with little or no relative content, you will find yourself very near the end of the list of hits that the search found.

You can see how important optimization of your site for search engines really is. So how do you help your chances with a search engine? Although no webmaster knows for sure, there are some things that most people agree are good, solid techniques to employ.

Content – everyone agrees on one thing: content is king. With all the theories and speculations on how search engines rank sites, at the end of the day the most important thing for any engine is to deliver relevant results to the user. Building a content-rich website will not only help with your search engine placement, but will give your visitors a positive experience and keep them coming back.

Focus – it's not only important to have good content, but to keep it focused as well. If your website has information on tractors, greenhouses and baseball, the search engines will not know how to classify your basic page content. If you want to increase your chances for high ranking, there should be no ambiguity in your site's focus.

Graphics – we've already talked about how keywords in meta-tags are simply ignored, and in fact if a word is repeated too many times on the page it can be detrimental. There are legitimate ways to work in keywords used in various ways, though, and one of them is in the graphics on the page. Too many people don't give any thought to naming their graphic files; they call them pic1.jpg, pic2.jpg, pic3.jpg, etc. On a farm equipment page, it would be much better for the names to be specific, such as: tractor.jpg, hayrake.jpg, baler.jpg, etc. Be aware that there is an HTML option to give a description of the photo using the "alt" attribute so that if someone moves the mouse over it, the text is displayed. Both the name of the image and the description are available to search engines should they decide to use it. There is evidence that some do, because Google allows a search strictly for photos.

These are just a few techniques to try, and you can find other suggestions out on the web. Just be wary of any ways that people give you to "trick" the search engines – they simply don't work, and can actually hurt you. Also be wary of any service that promises to get your site close to the top of a search if you simply hire them, because there are many people out there hoping to make money off of website owners who don't really understand the internet.

Basically, just create a good site with tons of useful content relative to your topic and submit it to the search engines – you will get some traffic. How much traffic depends on how hard you work to add content and improve your site for maximum rating.

That's an oversimplification and there are hundreds of companies and SEO professionals working in this field that struggle to get good position...but it's the only game in town...to get traffic you need a good site!

Driving Traffic To Your Site

Another way to get traffic to your site is to drive it there. Like herding cattle, you have to round up interested prospects and drive them to your site where they can wander around, read the information, develop an interest in you and your book, and even click the magic button and buy a copy.

I use an integrated approach to this. First of all, I make sure that I have a nice, professional site; well constructed, full of useful content, and with a shopping cart for orders. Then I use the website address – the URL – in all of my promotions and advertising. I also keep the URL link in my signature line of my email and any other internet posting. That way if someone sees a posting in a discussion group or a comment on a blog that I've written, the viewer can click on that link and get immediately taken to my site. There they can snoop around, read my content and perhaps bookmark me for future visits. They can also choose to buy my book, ask a question, or go to my blog and read/comment on my postings there.

What all this means is traffic. You can generate traffic and create interest in you and your book by participating in something called the "social media." It's really a community of like-minded people with a shared interest that come together in certain online forums to read and talk about their topics. These are passionate people with a strong interest, and to make it better, they really enjoy meeting their peers.

There are hundreds of social media sites that are popular right now; sites like Facebook, Myspace, Twitter, Tumblr, etc. A simple search of those terms will bring you enough information to keep you busy for a long, long time. Each one is different, with different rules, so be sure to study the sites and know what you are doing before participating. The possibilities are endless.

There is one thing that is paramount when dealing with any social media forum, and this is extremely important. Never, ever, ever try to sell something there – it means instant death! You will get flamed, blasted, torn to ribbons, humiliated and barred from future participation.

The social media sites were created to share information and exchange ideas with people very much like you. But if you just jump in without exploring 'niche' world and simply try to BS your way along, you will get caught and the bad things will happen; your experience will be over before it even starts. You have to be real, knowledgeable, have a genuine interest in the subject, and know something about it and offer helpful and meaningful information.

The upside is this: If you are genuine and participate in these forums and discussions, and if you attract interest, they will automatically track you down and come to your site. They do that because they like what you have to say and want more. If your site is full of content and resources and you also offer a book for sale, then guess what? That's right, you will sell books.

By joining the social media community and participating instead of selling, you will attract traffic, drive them to your site, and make sales. Best of all, it can all happen while you are sitting at your desk at a day-job, or laying on the beach getting a tan. It's the internet... silent, and never resting.

Pay-Per-Click Advertising

The other day I was watching television, and the show cut to a commercial break. Sometimes I use such an opportunity to go to the restroom, grab a bottle of water out of the refrigerator, or even surf through the other channels just to see what else happens to be on. This particular occasion, though, I watched the commercials, waiting for the program to return. One came up that grabbed my attention – it was for a new computer gadget that really caught my eye. I was intrigued enough that I walked over to my desk to do an online search for the item so that I could read more about it.

When I finally returned to my television program, I stopped to think how complicated the field of advertising must be. After all, the company didn't just have to create a commercial that would attract my attention and make me want to buy their product. They also had to run it in a time slot and during a program where people that would be interested in such a thing would be watching. There was also an element of luck involved, because I could have just as easily been in the kitchen peeling an apple to eat during the next segment of the show.

If you do a little research into the advertising world, you'll discover that there are specialists who do nothing but consult on when a particular type of product should advertise on TV. They understand the demographics of programs, keep up with the latest statistics, and watch trends in the industry. That's their niche in the business, and they are well-paid for what they do.

On the other hand, there are other people whose job it is to construct a commercial that will be appealing to a person who might by the particular product being advertised. They understand about the appeal and aesthetics of the visual medium, and know how to cram a powerful sales pitch into a thirty-second commercial.

Still others have special knowledge about how often the commercial should be repeated, and there are those folks whose job it is to take the finished product and expose it to test audiences to measure how effective it can potentially be.

Before a national commercial is run on television, an incredible number of people have already seen it, and hundreds of thousands – if not millions – of dollars have been spent on developing it.

None of this probably surprises you, but what I'm about to say next will... I'm going to suggest that you do something very similar by advertising your book on the internet, but you're going to do 100% of all the marketing and development of the ad by yourself. Sound intimidating? I'd be shocked if it didn't; hold on, though, because I think that you will be surprised how easy it is to dive into the world of pay-per-click advertising – hey, you may even have a good time with it!

While there are many pay-per-click advertising companies on the web, we're going to look at a very common one: Google AdWords. You've probably seen them everywhere on the web. As you surf different pages, you've no doubt noticed a column or row of advertisements proceeded by, "Ads by Google…" Those are a lot like the television ads that I just described.

Someone wrote each ad, decided the subject matter of the websites that they would be placed on, and pay for the positioning on the page. Unlike our earlier example of the television commercial, using AdWords is actually quite easy, and with a little testing like we discussed earlier, you can probably do quite well

Some people look at the AdWords program and see the complicated television commercial example that I mentioned. The key to using it successfully, though, is to understand the way that the program works… and actually it is quite simple.

It doesn't cost anything for an ad to be displayed on a target website. If someone viewing the site sees the ad and clicks on it, however, there is a cost incurred. The website viewer is taken to your website, and you are charged for the click. You decide how much you're willing to pay for each click when you first set up the program.

Let's look at a quick example using the theoretical book on how to build a greenhouse that we used earlier.

1. To begin with, you need a website from which you are selling the book.
2. To get the AdWords program going, you would write a small ad: "Build Your Own Greenhouse Now! An easy, step-by-step guide to creating your dream greenhouse."
3. Next, sign up for Google AdWords on their website.
4. Select the keywords to be associated with your ad – "greenhouse" springs to mind first, although "home gardening" might be a close second. Your ad can be displayed when someone does a Google search for that term, or goes to a website with that theme that displays Google ads.
5. It's now time to decide exactly how much you will pay for someone to click and visit your website – let's say, ten cents for example.
6. Determine how much you're willing to spend per day, and set that value next. If your budget is $30/month, and a month has an average of thirty days, then you wouldn't want to spend more than $1 per day. At ten cents per click, that means that you'd generate ten clicks per day.
7. Next, sit back and monitor the situation. If you are getting sales, then you're on the right track. On the other hand, if you're getting hits on the site but no sales, it means that your website may need some attention. If no one is clicking on your ad, it may need re-wording. By tweaking the parameters of the program and fine-tuning them, you may be able to generate sales for your book.

There are some finer points of the program to consider, though. The first thing is ad placement. If you go to Google.com with your web browser and put in the term "greenhouse," not only will you be given a list of resulting web sites, but you will also see a list of ads on the side of the screen. As you scroll through page after page of search results, the ads will change as well... so what determines which ad is displayed on the top of the first page, and which one is displayed at the bottom of the fifth page? Easy – the amount that each person decided to pay per click is used to arrange the ads, from the highest amount at the top, to the lowest at the bottom. If someone was to bid $0.25 per click on the term "greenhouse" and you bid $0.10, your ad would be displayed beneath theirs. If another fellow bid $0.05, then his ad would be displayed beneath yours. It's a lot like an auction – whoever "bids" the most gets the top position.

It is still a little more complicated than that, though. Using those same numbers, if the top ad fellow had configured to pay no more than a total of $0.75 per day for all clicks to his site, then after the third time that his ad was clicked on at $0.25 per click, it would roll off and the one below it would take the number one position.

If you remember the section on testing your marketing/sales program, that concept is just as important here. If you are spending more than you're bringing in through sales, then you definitely need to tweak your AdWords program. Just like the table of results and corrections that was presented in that section, here's one that specifically addresses your AdWords campaign:

Result	Correction Needed
People aren't clicking on your ad	Either the ad needs re-wording because it isn't enticing them to click, or a low bid is causing poor placement and no one sees it
People click on the link, costing you money, but they aren't buying the book	The website sales letter and/or price needs tweaking

After you manipulate your ad and sales site and drive both to a steady sales pace, however, then you can reap the true rewards of the AdWords program. You can collect the checks from your sales every month!

Added Income Using AdSense

We just discussed the AdWords program; on the reverse side of the coin is the AdSense program, also hosted by Google. This puts you on the other side of the equation, though – instead of advertising your product, you are allowing Google to place ads on your website for other pages and sites.

With AdWords, you were bidding to get placement for your ads, but with AdSense, people are bidding to get their ads on your site. The best news is that Google pays you every time that someone clicks on one of the ads.

This can be a two-edged sword, however – if you have a website advertising a book on a particular subject but also include AdSense ads on that subject, you are allowing advertisers to entice people away from your website.

It is an easy process to sign up for; simply go to google.com, click on "advertising programs," and select AdSense. You will use the same account for both AdWords and AdSense, so if you've signed up for one, you're immediately ready to use the other. Once you're on the AdSense site, you can use a tool to generate the HTML code to place on your website where the ads will be displayed.

There are some rules to be aware of, and the first is about website content. The content on your website cannot relate to violence, racism, pornography, illegal drug use, gambling, weapon sale, alcohol sale, or any content that promotes illegal activity. There are several other restrictions that are spelled out on the Google website, so be aware of them. At first glance you might think, "Of course I have an above-board website – that won't be a problem for me!" Consider the case of a friend of mine, though. He used AdSense to generate revenue on both his business and personal websites. The family website had content that you could imagine: hobbies, interests, vacations, etc. On the vacation page he had a list of places that they had been in the last few years, each with their own sub-page: San Francisco, Natchez, Savannah, and Las Vegas, to name a few. They stayed at the Mirage Hotel & Casino on the Vegas trip, and had all sorts of photos and trip notes on the page. Guess what, though… no matter what the context, the webpage was about a casino, which could have gotten his AdSense account suspended, or even cancelled. He realized this before Google caught the violation, and he quickly removed the code for AdSense on the Vegas vacation page.

Content isn't the only thing that Google polices, though. Clicking your own ads to generate revenue will get you tossed right out of the AdSense program. When someone clicks on an ad from your site, their address information is captured and long-term trends are analyzed. For example, if you go to a friend's site and click on the ads several times a day the repetition will be noticed, and Google will take action to stop the fraudulent behavior.

You can't even encourage clicks on your website. It is against the rules to have anything that says, "Click on my ads to support my site," or even "Click here for some cool information." AdSense will display "Ads by Google" at the top of the advertisements that it puts in, and that's all that is allowed.

There are a few more rules, but the bottom line is that if you want to have Google ads on your site, sign up with the program, add the HTML code that they provide to your website, and then sit back and let it happen.

That brings us back to the big question: to use AdSense ads on your site to try to generate revenue, or not to use them so that your visitors will remain focused solely on your product.

Personally, I take two approaches. The first one is if I am using a one page website that's primarily a hard-hitting sales letter for my book, I probably won't have any AdSense content on it. I focus on driving people to the site who are already interested in my topic, so I don't use any Google Ads on the page.

The second approach is when I have a book with deep back-end appeal with other products and services. The website a bit more complicated, and I will have some AdSense content there, as well as some other books for sale via my Amazon affiliate program. I'll offer some of the other products and services as well. With a site like that, I'm trying to build an email list and keep them coming back, which makes the AdSense clicks easier to accept.

You will have to decide which one works best for your particular situation, but do remember what I said a while back about testing your strategy – if the Google ads aren't generating any revenue, they're easy to take off the page. If they are bringing in a tidy little sum, then you may want to make your site deeper with more pages, and therefore more ads. Like anything else in marketing and sales, it's all about tweaking your strategy to achieve maximum performance.

Viral Marketing

"Viral marketing" certainly doesn't sound that attractive… in fact, if someone came up to me, extended his hand, and said, "Hi, I'm a viral marketer!" I doubt that I'd want to shake it. Viral marketing just doesn't sound that, well, safe and sanitary.

Actually, though, if done correctly it is a powerful marketing tool in this internet age. The term was first used by Jeffrey Rayport, a Harvard Business School professor, in his 1996 article *The Virus of Marketing*. It refers to a marketing program that spreads by word of mouth like a virus, usually over the internet.

I was party to a viral marketing strategy not long ago. It all started when a friend emailed me about a hilarious website called "Subservient Chicken." She raved about what a hilarious website that it was, and to me (and all her other friends in her address book) to go check it out.

I pointed my web browser to **www.subservientchicken. com**, and the Burger King logo came up with the phrase, "Contacting the chicken…" What happened next is pure internet magic – a living room was shown on a photo in the middle of the screen, and a guy in a chicken suit walks into the picture. He stands there, as if waiting to be commanded, and it appears though you are watching him on a webcam. A text-entry box underneath reads, "Get chicken just the way you like it. Type your command here." As it turns out, this is just a way – albeit an extremely clever one – to get the word out about Burger King's Tendercrisp Chicken Sandwich, which is mentioned on the page with a click-ad. But the thing that keeps you there is that you can type in commands for the chicken to do, and for the most part, he'll do them. It looks like Burger King filmed the chicken doing everything that they could think of, and then used some word-mapping software to link various phrases to different behaviors. Here are some popular things that people have the chicken do: sneeze, riverdance, watch TV, read a book, die, etc.

It's extremely silly, but you'll find yourself mesmerized with making the chicken do things. I have to say that this was brilliant – because after you finally tire of ordering the chicken around, the next thing that you do is immediately email all your friends and tell them about the subservient chicken. Word spreads like a virus. You tell ten people, they each tell ten people, each of them tell ten more, etc.

This clever ad campaign was conceived for Burger King by the advertising agency of Crispin, Porter, and Bogusky. I don't know how long the site will remain up, but as of this writing it is still there. I know this because I just went to check it out, and spent several minutes thinking of things for the chicken to do such as lay an egg, stand on the couch, do jumping jacks, and others that I just lost track of. This site is a perfect example of viral marketing.

There are several aspects that define viral marketing:
- You give away something free. In the case of the subservient chicken, it is a chance to interact with the website without cost.
- It is something new and attractive. The chicken idea was genius, and had never been done before. If I were to launch my own "subservient eagle" website, it would probably be vastly ignored.
- It is easy for people to spread around. Pre-internet, when the FAX machine ruled the business world, you may remember the old habit people had of faxing cartoons and jokes to their friends. The internet has simply made that process easier, which is how the chicken spread – people simply emailed the link to friends.
- Has something that attracts people, or contains something that they want. Everyone wants to laugh and be entertained, which is what made the chicken so wildly popular.
- As word spreads about the item being marketed, it ads little or no cost to the originator. In our example, once the subservient chicken site was in place, it didn't cost Burger King anything extra whether one person or one million people viewed it.

Successful viral marketing depends on keeping the ball rolling; if people don't continue passing the word along, then the campaign will fizzle. Unfortunately, I can't tell you how to do a successful viral marketing campaign for your particular book – there is no specific formula, only the guidelines and description that I listed above. You will have to decide if this type of marketing can work for you, and then explore possibilities that complement your product.

What might be of help, however, is to examine several examples of successful viral marketing campaigns that might help provide inspiration and get your ideas flowing.

The Blair Witch Project

I must stand up and give these folks a round of applause. They made a low-budget film in a way that had never been done on such a scale before, and then sent its profits through the roof by using viral marketing.

Basically, this was a movie about three college kids who go out into the New England woods to search for the legendary "Blair Witch." Filming was done by the actors as if they were doing their own cheap documentary, and it had a surprise ending where all three disappeared. The marketing that was spread by a website and by word of mouth was that their film had been discovered out in the woods, and that was what was being shown at the theaters… the big question, "Is it real???" made everyone tell their friends about the movie, and it was a phenomenon. Even if you didn't like the movie, as a marketing person you must admit that it was a brilliant twist to releasing a film.

Get "Simpsonsized"

Speaking of movies, when the Simpsons movie was released in 2007 Burger King was a partner in marketing, and they put up a website called "simpsonizeme.com" where you could upload a photograph of yourself, and it the website would turn you into a Simpsons character. Of course, you could email it to all your friends, and they would in turn have to "Simpsonize" themselves and sent out the photo, and so on. It promoted not only the new Simpsons movie, but also the movie tie-in promotions at Burger King.

The Million Dollar Homepage

This is an example of something that could have simply fizzled, but didn't. The entrepreneur was taking a chance that it would take off, and since the risk/investment was very low, it was worth giving it a try. A gentleman put up a website with a grid of one million pixels (those tiny dots that make up graphics on the screen) and set out to sell them for a dollar each – with the guarantee that the site would be up for at least one year. The story was that he wanted to try to make a million dollars to pay off his student loans and have some money in the bank to get started. He launched his website, and the news picked it up – before long he was in print media, on broadcast television, and hits to his site were escalating. At that point, commercial ventures such as Golden Palace Online Casino starting buying ads to ride the wave of publicity. It wasn't long until he had sold all 1,000,000 pixels and was a millionaire.

Remember that one of the aspects of viral marketing is that it is new and unique, because several people came along after him and tried to do the exact same thing… and fell flat on their faces. Only the first guy got the bucks and the publicity.

Get Your Free Email Here

There's probably no better example of viral marketing than Hotmail. This internet company started offering free email – all you have to do is register. The one thing that they do is to add a line at the bottom of each email that you send promoting their service. It's one, unobtrusive line that most people don't object to at all, especially since they're getting free email service:

"To get your FREE email account goto www.hotmail.com"

So what happens? Well, if you're a Hotmail user, then your friends and associates all see the advertisement at the bottom of your emails, and some of them click and sign up for their own free email account. Their friends and associates see the ad at the bottom of their emails, and some of them click and sign up… see how word about Hotmail spread like a virus? They do much more than just email, but getting everyone to sign up for a free account rapidly built their customer base. Now they can change the advertisement line at will to highlight different aspects of their service. For example, I just saw one of their new taglines:

Need to know the score, the latest news, or you need your Hotmail – get your "fix"

Hotmail.com continues to be a leader in the world of viral marketing.

What are your chances of surviving a zombie apocalypse?

This last example may be one of my favorites, because not only is it a fun and unique little site, but it also indirectly pre-qualifies visitors for the advertisement that will be shown.

The site is an online dating service, and the URL that got emailed around madly is **http://www.oneplusyou.com/bb/ zombie**. The premise is based on the zombie movies such as "Night of the Living Dead," "Day of the Dead," "Dawn of the Dead," and even "Shawn of the Dead." Chances are that no one who's ten years old or seventy years old will be taking the quiz, because those icons aren't part of their popular culture. No, the people who take this quiz are either in the young adult dating, or second-time-around dating age. Basically, you are asked fifteen questions that are entertaining enough by themselves, such as:

In the event of a zombie apocalypse, would you drive 20 minutes across town to find your loved ones?
1. Yes, they're probably in trouble and I must save them
2. No, they've probably turned into zombies or are dead

When you've taken the short quiz and your answers are being tabulated, you are taken to a website offering free membership in an online dating service sponsored by a company called Mingle2. Although outright commercials aren't generally part of successful online marketing, this one is very unobtrusive and you can easily click, "No, let me see the results."

The idea of how you would fare in a worldwide zombie attack is fascinating enough that this simple quiz was forwarded all around the country. It is just downright fun, and takes no time. When I took it I learned that my probability of surviving a zombie apocalypse is only 52%. Let's hope that it never happens!

To wrap up our discussion on viral marketing, remember that I said I couldn't tell you exactly how to do it – that's because specific rules simply don't work in that arena. Once something has been done, it becomes immediately obsolete. The next viral marketing success will be someone who comes up with something new and unique. I can give you a few pointers to steer you in the right direction, though.

1. You must evoke emotion! After experiencing your creation, be it a website, filmclip on youtube, etc., the viewer must be driven to *immediately* tell all their friends and email a link to it to everyone that they know.
2. Don't simply build an advertisement and think that it's going to work. Regular marketing is perfect for telling people how miraculous your book is, but viral marketing is not the time for a standard commercial. Even with the zombie apocalypse website were there was a blatant ad, it was given only as an afterthought – the main focus, including the questions, artwork, and results were all about surviving the zombies… which is what made people flock to it in the first place.
3. Make it easy to share. Most successful viral marketing campaigns have an "email to a friend" link. The magic happens when people start sharing it with their friends, so make that as easy as possible, and available in as many ways as possible.
4. Never, never, never restrict access to your viral marketing campaign. You may require people to give their email address to get your ezine, but if you're trying a viral marketing campaign, it should be free, easy, and unrestricted.

I hope that those tips help – viral marketing is a tricky world to operate in, and one that is new and relatively unchartered... which can make it all the more attractive.

Affiliate Marketing

When you're thinking about marketing, do you ever wish that you had a sales force that would go out and find new and creative ways to promote your book? Well, believe it or not, such a concept isn't outside of your grasp – people are out there who are anxious to sell your product... and it won't cost you a dime unless they're successful.

The concept is called "Affiliate Marketing," and a lot of people have done quite well by incorporating it into their sales model.

Here's the basic concept:
1) A person (an "affiliate") advertises your book on his or her website.
2) A visitor to the site sees it, and purchases the book.
3) You receive payment, and ship the book directly to the buyer.
4) You pay the affiliate a commission on the sale.

It sounds easy and straightforward, and to be honest, it can be. But affiliate marketing is also one of those things that can be as difficult and complicated as you want to make it. A friend of mine used a shopping cart system that automatically tracked affiliate sales, and it was done effortlessly and painlessly... it was also about a hundred bucks a month.

Still, you must have some way of managing your affiliates. Imagine having a dozen people who've signed up as affiliates, all linking to your website, and an order comes in. There's no way to know which affiliate's website sent the customer to your order page, and with multiple order rolling in, the whole process would be a nightmare to track and maintain.

Thankfully, there are many solutions out there, ranging from freeware that may be require a little more work on your part (and a little patience with software that hasn't been extensively tested), to deluxe systems that do everything imaginable – but cost more. We'll talk more about choosing an affiliate package in a moment. Before that, there are some basics to cover.

SETTING YOUR COMMISSION

Affiliate programs exist for goods and services all across the internet – everything from books, to logo design. How much each program pays varies according to many factors that include the final price of the item, and the profit margin for the seller. High-priced items offered by national manufacturers may pay as low as 1% to the seller, while something with a high profit such as an ebook may bring up to 50% for the referrer.

The first thing that you need to do is to determine how much you're going to pay one of your affiliates when he sells a copy of your book. Making the decision is like wielding a two-edged sword; you want to retain as much of the profits for yourself as possible, but also you want to entice your affiliates to promote and sell your product. If an affiliate is setting up a website to push products, and your book will bring them $1/unit but another book will bring $4/unit, which one will probably get preferential treatment? That's right, the one that brings in the most money. Let's therefore look at a few pricing examples to keep in mind, using a retail price of $20 for your book (to keep the math easy):

- You'll make the most profit with you sell the book in person; if each book costs you $3 to print, then each time someone buys your book directly you pocket $17 – no packing, no shipping, no other direct charges.

- If someone buys your book from your website, then you'll incur shipping charges, payment collection charges (from your credit card company, PayPal, etc.), and some nominal amount for your web presence. Let's say that all adds together for a total of $3.50 in charges for that sale. Add that to the $3 for the book, and that leaves you a total of $13.50, which is still a healthy profit.

- Selling your book in a bookstore may or may not be something that you're planning on or even interested in, but typically a retail establishment will want a 50% discount, and you'll have to pay to send your book to them. In this example, the bookstore will pay you $10 per book. Shipping will vary depending on how many books you can send at once, but let's make it easy and call it a buck. Add the $3 cost of the book, and you'll make $6 when someone picks up your book.

- Amazon Createspace is a wonderful self publisher's option. They print your book 'on demand' and ship it to your customer. They will pay you about 45% of the cover price and the customer pays for shipping. (**www.createspace.com**).

This table sums up everything that we've just talked about regarding a book sale and using the example of a $20 cover price:

	In Person	Website	Bookstore	Amazon. com
Profit	$17.00	$13.50	$6.00	$9.00

The total income that you generate will be a combination of all of the above, and I wouldn't discourage any stream of income. For someone to see your book in a store and buy it represents a sale that you might not have gotten otherwise. Even though it's not your biggest profit margin, it's money that you wouldn't want to turn down – and that's exactly how I think of sales through affiliate programs.

Most affiliate programs pay a commission of anywhere from 5% to 15% of the sale price, so continuing with the $20 book example for easy math, it is simple to see how that would affect your profit based on the website profit that we already calculated above:

Commission %	Commission $	Profit
5 %	$1.00	$12.50
10 %	$2.00	$11.50
15 %	$3.00	$10.50
25 %	$5.00	$7.50

You can see that even paying a commission of 15% yields a higher profit than a bookstore sale – a full 75% more. Even giving a commission of 25% gives you a better margin than either a book sold by a retail establishment... and keep in mind, the only time that you pay is when a book is sold and you have the money in your hand. What's the message here? Well, it is simply that the numbers add up – an affiliate program can be worth the time and effort to get it started.

Setting up an affiliate program

You can hire affiliate networks such as Commission Junction and Be Free (both now owned by ValueClick), LinkShare or Performics. They handle the tracking and money – and charge you a healthy percentage. Those companies charge a few thousand dollars to get your affiliate program established.

Social Media Marketing

There's a new term that has been bantered about quite a bit lately – "social media." It refers to a concept that's been around for a while, where the internet is used for sharing information and discussing various topics with other people. I'm sure that you've heard of some of the more popular sites: Facebook, MySpace, etc. There are new social media websites springing up every day.

Social media, or social networking, gets its name from the fact that humans contribute to the content of the site. This could be in the form of a blog where comments and postings can be added, an informational site such as Wikipedia whose content comes directly from users, or a community of people that link and exchange information through their own pages like Facebook.

People exchange information on everything: hotels, movies, restaurants, literally anything that you can imagine. This has been catching some folks completely off guard, and many don't know how deal with the fact that their company or business is being discussed online.

For example, in August of 2008 something very interesting happened on the social media website Twitter. One of the most popular television shows at that time was the American Movie Channel (AMC) program "Mad Men," which enjoyed critical acclaim and an incredible fan base. AMC discovered that some people had set up Twitter identities as the main characters from Mad Men, and they were making posts in the guise of those characters. The AMC legal department immediately sent cease and desist notices to Twitter, demanding that the "character" accounts be disabled, citing the Digital Millennium Copyright Act and accused the social media site of being in violation. That was at 2:00 PM on August 26th, but by 6:45 PM that same day the interesting thing happened... someone at AMC must have wandered into the legal department and pointed out that some of the "character" accounts had gathered nearly a thousand followers in only one week, and there was a new season starting up. AMC quickly contacted Twitter again, and gave them the legal equivalent of, "You know, maybe we were a little hasty in our decision." They green-lighted Twitter to put the accounts back up and reveled in all the free publicity that the show was getting on Twitter.

Now, you probably won't get the same social media marketing for your book, because you're not on national television. There are ways that you can use this outlet for promotion, however – so how do you use social media to sell your book? First, do some research and determine your knowledge niche, something that you can claim expertise in. It would be even more beneficial if it happened to be the topic of your book. Next, find a social media website and locate a group (or groups) of people with the same interest, that are meeting and discussing the subject. For example, if your niche happens to be 'ghosts,' then find other people interested in the supernatural and join their community. When you sign up, you are usually able to add a signature for your posts, or some general information about yourself – make sure that you include your website as part of the general info.

Now this is extremely important: never, ever, ever try to sell anything. Just join the conversation. It's okay to share stories or experiences, answer questions, ask questions, and generally become part of the group. You should never post "Well, in my latest book…" Take your time, don't be in a hurry, and do good things to add to the conversation. Contribute worthwhile and meaningful information to the group and you'll become noticed and appreciated.

What will happen, after you become known and have proved that you are genuine and have useful information, is that people will do some quiet research and find your site and visit. They may do a google search and read about you. They will find out that you are a published author on the subject, and maybe even get a hit on your books for sale on Amazon.com.

Participation will bring traffic, which in turn will bring volume of sales. It will grow as people spread the word amongst themselves. That's the viral aspect of the social network – people share what they think is good.

So, with a book, a website, a shopping cart, and a willingness to spend some time developing your network and your list, you could drive traffic to your website, enhance your sales, and gain some notoriety in the process.

Discussion groups/Forums

Discussion groups and forums are websites where you can read current topics (called "threads"), and then add your own comments to the discussion. People will then read your post, and add their thoughts on what you had to say. As you may have already guessed, this is simply another form of social media, but it has been around for a long time. In fact, this concept predates even the web, when the internet was focused on newsgroups known as the "Usenet." Today, there are many online discussion forums on websites that cover any topic imaginable. I would give you the same advice that I did when using any social media outlet:

- Don't sell your book, or try to crowbar it into conversation. You'll get flamed, ignored, or removed from the discussion.
- Choose a discussion group or forum that is relevant to your book topic.
- Make sure that you have your website clearly displayed in your signature file that is attached to all of your postings, but don't call attention to it. Never enhance it with a phrase like, "click here for more information on this discussion!!!"
- Finally, your website needs to have information that participants in the forum will find useful, interesting or helpful when they visit. You should then have a clear path to a purchase link to buy your book.

By following those simple rules, you can turn the turn the discussion groups and forums into a powerful marketing tool.

Blogs and Blogging

The term "blog" comes from the name "web log," and basically started out as online logs, or diaries. When a person wrote a blog (known as "blogging") he or she posted their comments and thoughts on a regular basis – usually either daily, or weekly at the most. If you wonder how popular blogs are, consider the fact that by the end of 2007, the blog search engine Technorati was tracking more than 112 million blogs.

By now, you've probably already guessed what I'm going to say next – yes, blogging is simply another form of social media. With most blogs today, readers can add their own comments, more readers can comment on theirs, and so on, and so on.

The same social media marketing rules apply from the previous sections – if you use your blog to pound advertisements for your book down people's throats, they will realize that and – as the old saying goes – stay away in droves.

The great thing about blogs is that they are usually on a standard webpage format, which means that you can have ads to support your blog. You can use Google AdSense (like we discussed in the pay-per-click section) to generate revenue, or you can directly post ads for your book.

Now, if all this sounds like a daunting task, don't worry. There is a site that ready to help you launch into the world of blogging: **www.blogger.com**. You can get set up for free, name your blog, and even choose a pre-defined style. You won't believe how easy it is.

But there is a hard part – posting your comments on a regular basis. I'd guess that ninety percent of the people who start a blog do it the exact same way: the first we they post a couple of times a day. By the second week, it's down to once a day. At the month mark, a day gets skipped every now and then. When two or three months roll around, though, postings only come on a weekly basis… and it deteriorates from there. No one thinks that this will happen on their blog because they are so excited about it at the start. Believe me, blogging becomes a job.

I have a friend who regularly does 10K runs – basically, that's 6.2 miles. As many as he's done, he says that every one is basically the same. The first mile is a breeze, and he's thinking, "hey, I might even win this race!" When the second mile marker comes around, he says that he's starting to notice a slight pain in his legs. By mile four the pain is real, and he is wondering if he can hold out for two more miles. And by the sixth mile, he is usually struggling and praying to make the next two-tenths. Now, when the race is over he's drinking down a bottle of cold water, people are patting him on the back, and he tells me that he feels like a million dollars. The point is though, that the further along he is in the race, the tougher it is.

That's *exactly* what blogging is like. If you start down this road, make up your mind that you are going to stick with it and post regularly, because that is what will make people read your blog, post their thoughts, and keep them coming back.

Video and Audio Features

In today's high-tech world, audio/visual enhancements are the order of the day for websites. In your daily surfing I'm sure that you are used to seeing all those things. For example, I happened to catch part of the NASCAR race last Sunday, and because of a rivalry between two drivers, there was an intentional wreck after the checkered flag had flown. The next day I went to the sport's website, **www.nascar.com**, and they had a video replay of it that I watched several times.

The thing about it is that I expected it to be there – I was interested to see it, but the fact that it was online was no big deal. Ten years ago I would have thought that it was some type of sorcery, because the technology wasn't even conceivable back then.

Today it is commonplace – as you have no doubt noticed. Fortunately, it's also become quite simple to employ this technology on your own website. First and foremost, you have to get a good quality digital recording, whether you are using audio or video. While renting a recording studio and contracting with an engineering staff to produce your content might be preferable, it's simply not realistic for most people. The cost would completely blow the budget and destroy profit margins.

There is thankfully a low-cost alternative... just do it yourself!

For audio, hand-held digital recorders can work well – the technology has come a long, long way. Not long ago I was recording an audio clip with such a device, an Olympus WS-110 Digital Voice Recorder to be exact, and everything in the house was perfectly quiet. When I started recording my clip, I heard a train blow its whistle in the distance; of course, I assumed that it was so low and far away that the little hand-held recorder wouldn't pick it up. Guess what happened when I replayed the audio? That's right – not only was my voice crisp and clear, but there was the train in the background. Those digital audio recorders have become truly amazing.

The same thing is true for digital video recorders. With a little forethought, planning, and the help from a friend, you can produce a video clip that will work well for your website. Determine what you want to say, what the background will be, how you will be dressed, but most importantly, why someone would keep watching it once they click on the play button.

In the case of both audio and video digital recorders, you will find a USB port that plugs directly into your computer and makes the device look basically like a disk drive. You can copy the audio or video file onto your hard drive, and you're almost ready to upload it to your website.

The one other item that you will need is some type of playing software to make it easy for visitors to your site to use. There are many available, and a simple websearch will reveal an entire list to choose from. I've used products from **www.wimpyplayer.com** before and I've been very happy with the results. Their "Wimpy Button" provides a single button for a visitor to click on to play your message, and as of this writing it is only $19.95. They also make video and MP3 players for your website, all under $40. I wish that they would change the name of their website, since it doesn't inspire confidence, but I never have a problem remembering it… and that's probably what they're going for.

Most of these type products will have a small program file that you upload to your web server with your audio/visual clips, and then also have a few lines of HTML code for your web page that makes the magic happen. It's quick and painless, and will greatly enhance the experience of a visitor to your site.

Before leaving the world of A/V, I'd be remiss if I didn't mention the web's premier video sensation, youtube.com. It is basically a community where people post their own videos of all types. Some are silly, a few are downright offensive, but you'd be surprised how many people are using it for marketing. You can certainly upload your video to YouTube and then simply link to it from your website, and you would get the added bonuses of having it there. Probably the top two are the fact that it would be included in YouTube's database of video clips, and also you'd inherit the way that the site makes video sharing and referring simple. YouTube is probably best used for viral marketing, so if you have something that fits what we talked about back in that chapter, then youtube.com is definitely something that you should explore. It has an extensive help section that will get you started.

INTEGRATED MARKETING

Integrated marketing is simply the process of mixing conventional, direct marketing and new age internet marketing. Now, the first question that might spring to mind is… Why? With all the new internet technology that we have available, why in the world would anyone go back to any older sales methods?

The answer is simple… people are different. Even in today's world, some folks are completely unfamiliar with the internet. With all the talk of identity theft, others wouldn't dare use their credit card online – even on a secure site. Of course, the same person might hand their credit card to an unknown waiter or waitress at a restaurant, but that's beside the point. The important thing to consider is that the folks who won't order online are perfectly comfortable calling a toll-free number. You want your books to be available to everyone, no matter how they want to get them – so why not make it available through several methods?

Combinations

If you have a website, then there's no doubt that you should include the address (the URL) in every single piece of advertising you do, whether it's a print ad or a personal appearance on a radio program. Use the combination strategy everywhere, though. In a print ad make sure to highlight both your website and toll-free number. On your website, offer multiple ways to pay: credit card, e-check, and PayPal… but have snail-mail ordering information and your toll-free number there as well. Offering as many possibilities as you can will allow people to use whatever method is most comfortable to them, and will maximize sales.

Mix And Mingle Your Marketing

The same combination theory applies to your marketing as well as sales. To maximize your exposure don't just stick to whatever cutting-edge marketing strategy that you've just learned about. Do a combo of old-school and new-school methods. For example, get your website up and running as soon as possible, but also send out a press release to any media outlets that make sense. While you may be gearing up for tele-conferences put together from your email list, don't forget to schedule speaking gigs, conference appearances, and old fashioned book signings. In the sections that follow, we're going to look a little closer at several ways to use these additional marketing opportunities.

Book Signings

Book signings can be wonderfully successful, or brutally bad. They're easy to set up, since most bookstores have a community relations manager whose job it is to set up events for the public. Contact them, find a date that works for both of you, and you're ready to go... well, almost. Here are a few tips to help turn your signing into a profitable event.

- When you set up the book signing, use the three-call rule: call to book the signing, call one week before to verify it, and call the day of the signing to make sure that they have your books and are expecting you.
- Send invitations to anyone and everyone that you've

ever met in the bookstore's area. And to anyone and everyone that your brother-in-law's cousin's best friend has ever met in the area. If you can find 100 people to invite to your book signing, you will see results – it works.

- Assume that you won't have anything but a bare table, and be ready to set your own stage. I always bring a backpack with a tablecloth and a couple of stand-up signs, and on some occasions, depending on the book, I've brought a few props. Sometimes the bookstore has everything set up wonderfully for me, but other times I'll show up and they'll say, "Oh, was your signing today?" Roll with the punches, but be ready to do your own set-up.

- Stand, don't sit. Don't wait for the people to come to you... be there in the aisle to talk to them. Say hello as people walk by. Of course, the other half of this is to not be too pushy. I was doing a signing at one store and the manager told me a horror story about a guy who moved his signing table to the front door and ambushed everyone coming in, insisting that he sign a book for them. The manager told me that for weeks afterward, she found signed copies of his book stashed all over the store like Easter eggs – no one wanted it, yet he was forcing it on them! When you're at the signing, put yourself in the customer's shoes. If you walked into the store and some author grabbed you, insisting that you look at his book, what would you do? Most of us would probably run away. On the other hand, if you passed an author's table and she was sitting meekly behind her stack of books, you probably wouldn't give her a second glance. It's an art form, but walk that fine line between being invisible and annoying.

- Check with the store manager before bringing food. There are many stores invoking new policies that require that any food brought into the store be prepared by professional kitchens – it's a lawsuit protection thing. Just check it out before baking a plate of brownies to serve your guests.
- Above all, have fun. I've done signings where I sold one book, and others where I've sold over a hundred. The store manager's job is to make sure that everyone is having fun, and therefore wants to come back to the shop. Your goal should be to interact with customers, talk to the manager, and leave the store after the signing in the exact same manner whether you sold one copy or a hundred. After all, you want to come back there and sign again.
- When it's all over and you're driving home, do a post-mortem. If the signing wasn't a success, stop and think about what went wrong. Wasn't there anyone in the store during your time period? Did people pass your table by, but weren't interested? Ask yourself questions that relate to your signing, and use any bad experience as an information base to turn your next signing into a success!

Radio and Television

Radio interviews can be one of the most powerful avenues of publicity that you'll find – yet so many people live in dread of getting on live radio. Once you've done a few, you'll discover that they're fairly easy. They won't start out that way, though... if you're like everyone else, you'll be terrified. There are a few simple points that can help anyone become a radio pro, though.

- Landing interviews isn't as mysterious as you might think. Radio show producers have the job of booking interesting guests on the program. Now that certainly doesn't mean you can automatically get on their program just by asking, but present yourself in an interesting way you certainly stand a chance.

- If talking to a large group of people scares you, forget the audience! You know this if you've done radio before, but the vast majority of all interviews occur in the privacy of your home or office. You'll pre-arrange a time with the station, they'll call you, and it will be almost exactly like you're simply talking to someone on the phone. So many people get completely freaked out by the idea that thousands and thousands of people might be listening to the interview – but get a correct mindset to control this fear! Pretend that you're simply talking to a friend, or that there are only a handful of people out there. Once you get into the interview, and with a little experience behind you, it's easy to adopt that frame of mind... you're just talking to a friend on the phone.

- Try to work in regional information. Although it's not always the case, you'll usually have at least twenty-four hours to prepare. If there's some way that you can relate your book or interview topic to their region, chances are you'll get more airtime. Use the Internet to look up statistics or information pertaining to your discussion, and before the interview, work out a plan for weaving it into the conversation.

- Always be ready to go at a moment's notice. Once you've sent press kits and query letters to radio stations, they will keep the information in their files. One of the reasons for this is that if they need a last-minute guest, they'll have a large selection of guests at their fingertips. If this happens, though, you might get a last minute call saying, "Can you be on the air in 10 minutes?" If that happens, there can only be one answer: YES! If you work from notes, always have them in a file that you can access immediately. Personally, I don't; I just sit and mentally go over previous interviews, getting into the right mindset to get started right away. Whatever the case is with you, just be ready to be called for a last-minute performance.

- Get the details. When the producer of a radio show calls you to set up the interview, there are a few things that you have to write down. The first is the time... but just as important, the time zone. I've had the phone ring and someone say, "Okay, you're on in 5... 4... 3..." I'd say, "Wait! You said 9 AM!" The voice answered, "It is 9 AM – here on the east coast!" Learn how to calculate time zones if you don't already know. Also, be sure to ask how they found out about you. That will let you know which of your promotional avenues are working.

- Find out who you'll mainly be talking to – it's one more thing to ask during the set-up phone call. You'll also need to write down the exact names of all the persons you'll be speaking to in the interview. Although I've never had this happen, I have friends who spent an entire interview calling DeeJay James by the name "Johnny". Not a good thing. Find out who everyone on the show is, and how they want to be addressed.

- Send a free book to give away on the air. You will want to mention this during the set-up phone call as well, if there's enough time before the interview to get a book to them. Radio stations love to give things away to listeners, so if they can tie in a book giveaway with your interview, it can actually add time to your segment. I've used this technique many times, and it works well.

- Mention your book/website repeatedly. It is so easy to get lost in talking about the facts of an interview, and forget to mention your book name and/or website. If you over-mention them, it's going to turn off the interviewer and the audience, so try to strike a happy medium between not saying it at all, and bombarding the audience with it. My rule of thumb is that: if you think that you're saying it too much, you probably are. If you think that you're not saying it enough, you probably aren't.

- Be prepared for a call to go terribly wrong. No one wants this to happen, but it does. One of my best writer-friends in the world got a call to be on the "Snake and The Bruiser Show" in New York. When she started the interview, one DeeJay was serious and sincere, while the other asked the most horrid, irreverent questions. As it turned out, "Snake and The Bruiser" were shills from the Howard Stern show, and the entire thing was a terrible setup. While that extreme example probably won't happen to you, be prepared for some "shock jock" to turn on you at a moment's notice. Their mission is to offend you enough to get you to hang up the phone, which to be honest, you'll probably end up doing. Hang on as long as you can, answering offensive questions with "bypass answers" like, "Well, I don't know about that, but at mywebsite.com you can certainly find out about my book." Some people say that there's no such thing as bad publicity, so just hang on while you can, and get your name/website out there when you can.

- After the interview, send a thank-you email. Some folks swear that it should be a tangible, paper letter, but not me. We live in an electronic world, and producers keep electronic files. Send them an email, and they'll file it in their "great guest" mailbox (or wherever they keep their good information). Also, radio folks also have on-line industry bulletin boards where they list good guests, and sending a heart-felt "thank you" can help them remember to post your name there.

- If you can afford it, take out an ad in Radio-TV Interview Report (RTIR). I know that there's a lot of websites out there that promise to get you bookings and promotion, but RTIR is the real deal. It is sent to radio and television producers all across the nation – over 4,000 of them – and they all read it religiously. The folks at RTIR will help lay out your ad and make suggestions, so it's an easy process and one that is worth paying for. If you ask most anyone that's used RTIR, you'll probably hear incredible stories. An author friend of mine wrote a book named *A Ghost in My Suitcase*, and took out an ad targeted toward the latter part of the year. His results were incredible. While that's easy to say, I want to actually show you the places where he was interviewed over the course of just a month or so:

  11/22 - WKKX 1600 AM, The David Bloomquist Show, Pittsburg, PA

  11/01 - The X-Zone Radio Show with Rob McConnell, Syndicated U.S & Canada

  10/31 - WBNW 1120 AM, The Hire Frequencies Show, Boston, MA

  10/31 - KSLA-TV CBS, Shreveport, LA

10/31 - Michigan Talk Network (Syndicated Radio) hosted by Ryan Pritchard

10/31 - WTNK Radio 1090 AM, K.K. Wilson Show, Hartsville, TN

10/31 - WLTH 1370 AM, Mornings with Ron Muhammad, Gary, IN

10/28 - Louisana Live (Syndicated Radio) hosted by Don Grady

10/28 - KPFX 107.9 "The Fox", Fargo, ND

10/28 - KQDS 94.9 FM, Duluth, MN

10/28 - KRBE 104 FM, the Atom & Maria Morning Show, Houston, TX

10/27 - KSIR Radio, Fort Morgan, CO

10/27 - KVOX FM Froggy 99.9, Fargo, ND

10/27 - Mix 97.3 FM, The Ben & Patty Show, Sioux Falls, SD

10/26 - WSVA, THe Mike Schikman Show, Harrisonburg, VA

10/26 - WRRK Radio, John Nene, Pittsburg, PA

10/26 - Michigan Talk Radio Network (Syndicated Radio), Lansing MI

10/26 - KWRE Radio, "Live Wire" show w/ Mike Thomas, St. Louis, MO

10/24 - Magic 104 FM, The Cooper Fox Show, Conway, NH

10/24 - KDMX Mix 102.9, The New Morning Mix Show, Dallas, TX

10/21 - WICH 1310 AM, The Stu Bryer Show, Norwich, CT

10/18 - KQMT 99.5 Radio, "The Mountain", The Mark and Archer Show, Denver, CO

10/07 - WFAD Radio, The Jae Files, Middleburg, VT

I listed these for you because I wanted you to see the genuine results that can be obtained. Interestingly enough, although the locations range across the nation – yet he conducted every single interview sitting in his living room, parked in a comfortable rocking chair, in his hometown of Jefferson, Texas. RTIR can be an extremely powerful tool, and you can learn more about it at their website **www.rtir.com**.

Consulting

Many people use a consulting business to supplement their income, and there's nothing like a book to make you an "expert" on your chosen subject. Consulting basically breaks down to someone paying you to advise them using the information that you're already an expert on. It sounds easy, but there are some difficulties involved. Here are a few tips to be aware of:

- Be clear on what you are going to do – after all, you can't be all things to all people. It's important to define the scope of your consulting business. I know an author who wrote a book on dressing for success, and optimizing your closet. Not only does she sell her book when she gives talks to corporations, but she advertises her personal consultation business. When you hire her as a consultant, not only does she come to your home, organize your closet, and then take you shopping, but she also gives you a copy of her book to keep as a future reference.
- Network, network, network. It's important to find other consultants in your field, and network with them. You'll probably be surprised at how helpful they can be to you – most consultants know that there is plenty of business

out there, and by helping you, you can probably return the favor in the future after you have an established practice. And if you do receive help, never forget that – it is important that you return the favor in the future if anyone ever needs advise or assistance from you.

- Be in the right place at the right time. If your book has made you an "expert" on a specific topic, then find conferences and workshops in that arena that you can attend. Go as often as you can, and make it your job to meet as many people as possible there. You may even want to get a vendor table and sell your book – conferences and workshops are a wonderful place to spread your word.

- Give back when you can. If you are an expert at constructing home greenhouses and have written a book on that subject, use your skills to help others occasionally. Perhaps the local high school FFA could use your services on a project, or even your city's garden club. I'm a firm believer in the fact that when you give, you get back many times in return, so don't be stingy with your knowledge. Besides, it helps to spread your name around, and gets you publicity that you couldn't possibly buy.

- Be patient with your consulting business. If you're planning on using your book sales to make money, consulting can be a nice supplement. It takes time to build up business and a clientele, though. No matter how talented you may be, it takes time to get that first job, then the second, and even the third. Just hold on and keep plugging away, and you'll get there.

- You must promote yourself. After all, no one else is going to do it! As you're networking and looking for leads, remember to use every possible opportunity to promote yourself. Your consulting services can be touted in the same what that your book is – through a website, direct mail-out, etc. When it comes to consulting, I heard one expert on the subject say that beginning consultants should spend at least one-third of their time during their first year marketing their services, and the other two-thirds in actual billable time. After that first year, if things are going well, your marketing time can be reduced to 15-20 percent.

- Get ready for the valleys, as well as the mountaintops. As you're looking across the board at your income streams, if your consulting operation isn't comparing well with the others, give it time and attention. There are many people who make a good living as a consultant, but there are many more who use it to supplement their other income (such as book sales). Remember, your book makes you an expert in the field, and be sure to cross-promote your book sales and consultation business.

With all that said, be sure and remember that the consulting business is just an extra way to generate income using your book. It will fuel your book sales, and if promoted correctly, your book sales will fuel your consulting.

Speaking

If Speaking is a frightening word to you, you'll need to learn the importance and value that speaking to groups can really provide. There are tremendous benefits that come with it, but perhaps the most important one is having the ability to promote your book in the back of the room, where you can see substantial profit. If you add a sign up sheet for a free ezine or some other giveaway, you'll be automatically building your clientele list. Here are a few things about speaking to consider:

- Speaking gets your name out there. The more people who hear you speak, the more people there will be to purchase your book and refer you to other people are looking for professional speakers. Speaking at a meeting of a civic organization such as a Lions Club can lead to other jobs. You'll find that members of these organizations are in strategic positions in their business, and sometimes need to hire speakers and consultants.

- You will have the opportunity to sell your books at speaking engagements. Statistics clearly show that "back of the room" sales account for over 50% of professional speaking profits. You can promote your business and your book at the same time. You'll also be able to refer them to your website where they can get additional information, or even purchase your book. Face it, the more people that hear you speak, the more opportunities that you will have.

- Think three-dimensionally when it comes to your speaking engagements. Any such speech is an opportunity for you to create a videotape of your talk. You can use it not only to promote your speaking, but it can be used as a supplemental product on your website along with your book.

- Don't' forget that speaking gigs are a great place to network with people. You have to get your name out there, and speaking is a great way. After your speech, don't forget to mingle with your audience as well as the people who brought you there.

- Any speaking event is a great excuse to send out a press release. You can submit them to local newspapers and various online sites that have a "appearing in the area" section. It is a great way to get the word out about your book, your speaking career, and your consulting service.

The more that you speak, the more you'll learn how to use these events to promote yourself. You can turn them into future referrals and book sales. As you do this, more people will know about you and your book, and you'll be on your way to success!

Conventions, Trade shows and exhibits

I don't think that there's any better opportunity for promotion and sales than a gathering of your peers, so I would implore you not to pass up any chance to attend a convention, trade show, or exhibition that is within your expertise. It's a chance to meet like minds, make contacts, and just basically network.

Sometimes the price of admission can be negotiated. An author friend of mine recently contacted the vendor coordinator for a conference on the same topic as his book. Sales tables were $150 for the weekend, but he presented an interesting idea - if he could get a complementary table in prime position, he offered to donate $300 worth of his books for door prizes for the conference to give away during the meals and general times. The coordinator jumped on it, because it was such a great deal. It was an even better deal for my friend, though. His books sell for $19.95, so let's call it $20 to make it easy. To get the sales table, he had to donate 15 books to be used as giveaways for the conference, and they had a face value of $300. They only cost him $4 per book, though, so his expense was $60... he started out the conference by saving $90 on the cost of a sales table.

Remember what I said about networking earlier. There's no better place to do it than conventions, trade shows, and exhibits that showcase your area of expertise. Give your business card out to everyone you see - and make sure that it has a photo of the book cover on it. Of course, it should mention the fact that you do mentoring and speaking on the subject of your book as well.

Be a speaker! As long as you're there, find out who books the speakers, and strike up a conversation with him or her. Don't go high pressure, but do get the contact information so that you can send a speaking resume and possibly get on the agenda for the next year. If that happens, of course, you can certainly mention your book during your talk.

This last point is something that I've always thought about, but have never done. It does make sense to me, though. There's a wonderful conference called the Oklahoma Writer's Federation, Incorporated conference (OWFI), and I'm a big fan of it for many reasons. Probably the best aspect of the conference is that (at least in recent years) it is held in an Embassy Suites where everyone is all there together. Not only that, but everyone basically has a living room as well as a bedroom. Many speakers hold after-hours talk sessions in their living rooms, and these informal groups are announced at the conference every day. If I wasn't a speaker there, I'd still probably be tempted to print off signs saying, "Round-Table Discussion about <my topic> in Room 318 at 9:00

PM" and posting them on every floor, and by every elevator. I'd bet that would drive people to the discussion, and they'd become subscribers to my newsletter (or whatever marketing plan that I had).

The bottom line is that conferences and trade shows offer a world of opportunities for you and your book.

Becoming An Expert

Do you remember that old saying, "if it walks like a duck and quacks like a duck, then it must be a duck?"

That cliché definitely applies to being an expert in your field. If you have all the outwardly appearances of being an expert, then people will perceive you as one.

Here's an example – albeit a little odd one – that I was pondering just the other day. As I was watching the evening news, a story came on about the discovery of a dead bigfoot. They even had a photo of it shoved into a freezer. Now, things that are out of the ordinary immediately catch my attention, so I was immediately intrigued by the report. I watched with fascination as they interviewed first a zoologist, and then next a "bigfoot expert." After the story was over and the reporter moved on, I had to wonder what in the world made one an expert on a mythical beast. Not to slight bigfoot enthusiasts, but so far no one has produced a sasquatch alive or dead, so at this point the existence of such a monster is in question.

Getting back to that particular day, though, I just couldn't let go of the idea of a bigfoot expert. I did a quick web search for the fellow's name, and found out that he had a very extensive website on the subject. There were links to news reports about creature sightings around the country, film clips, and even a blog. You shouldn't be surprised about what I'm going to say next... he also had a book that he was selling on the site.

It then occurred to me that with a little time and effort, I could be a bigfoot expert right there in the comfort of my living room. How would I do it? Simple...

1. First I'd order a couple of the best-selling books on the subject from Amazon. I'd read them, digest the information, and look for any different angle on the subject that I might take.
2. I would get online and read every news story that I could find. Many newspapers have archives on the web that go back for years, so it should be an easy feat.
3. Next I'd sift through many of the existing bigfoot websites. I'm sure that there's be a lot of repetition, because when I did a quick search for the term "bigfoot" I got almost 13,000,000 results – yep, you read that correctly, there were nearly thirteen million pages. In my quest for knowledge I'd try to find the latest, most relevant ones and soak up the information that they had to share.
4. It would then be time to choose a topic for my bigfoot book, and I'd try to choose an angle that hadn't been done to death, basing that decision on the books that I read and my web research. I would then begin researching again, this time specifically for the topic that I'd selected. Maybe it would be "bigfoot physiology," or "rituals of the bigfoot creature," or even something

else – who knows. As I was digging through all the information, I would make notes for my book, and even be sketching out an outline.

5. Writing the book comes next, and I would attack it using the exact process that I described earlier in the "Write It" chapter. Of course, I'd follow the procedure of the "Publish It" chapter as well. While this wouldn't happen over night, I believe that I could be holding a bigfoot book within six months' time.

6. While I was waiting for the editing/layout/printing process to be completed, I would get my website up and running, and write a couple of reports to give away when visitors signed up to an ezine that I would start. I'd also get my sales page for the book ready to go, so that once I had book in hand I could go live immediately.

7. From there, I'd follow the points in this "Sell It" chapter – including contacting bigfoot conferences to get speaking gigs, getting in touch with talk radio stations, etc. The marketing campaign would begin in earnest.

Now, I'm sure that you've read this example with a smirk, thinking that I'm being a little tongue-in-cheek. To be honest, though, I would consider this a viable project. The fact that I got thirteen million hits off of a Google search tells me that there is a lot of interest in the subject out there. Hey, I'd be delighted to sell my book to a fraction of those with an interest in the subject. If I could sell an $18 book that costs me $4 to only 5,000 people, then I'd net roughly $70,000.00 – not to mention follow-on products and other ways to bring in money from being a "bigfoot expert."

Look For Events

Events are everywhere, and some authors get very creative in finding places to sell their books. Not just book signings at stores, mind you, but county fairs, flea markets, gun shows, craft fairs, you name it.

Just look around and find places where people are gathering for some sort of event, and you have a potential place to sell your books. I would caution you, however, to try to judge whether the crowd there would be receptive to your subject. For example, if your book is *The Evil of the Fermented Grape*, then I doubt you'd do well with it at a wine festival. On the other hand, if you were selling *The Wine Lover's Cookbook* then you'd probably move quite a few of them. Keep in mind that not every event is perfect for every book.

There are some common points about selling your books at events, though, and they are worth taking a quick look at:

1. Make sure the event organizers know that you're coming. With 99% of these things, there is some sort of reservation process to get a table. Sometimes you'll have to pay a fee, or it may simply be a matter of signing up. Follow the rules, though.
2. If the event has speakers and your topic would be a good fit, try to get on the agenda. Even if they don't pay, it could be worth the effort for increased book sales. You could always wave your speaker fee, or trade it for a sales table fee.
3. Always have handouts, bookmarks, business cards, or something to put in people's hands. Of course you'd prefer to sell a book, but even if someone doesn't want

to buy, you don't want a single person to leave empty-handed. Your giveway can contain information about the book, your web address, and any other contact information.

4. Treat the event organizers and staff well. They may be exhausted from hours of planning and dealing with people, so cut them some slack even if they're a little curt with you at times. You want to be remembered as the nice author who was there… and if you come back next time, that will be remembered.

5. Follow all the rules from the book signing section of this book – stand, don't sit; dress up your table; etc., etc., etc.

These are just a few suggestions for events where you make an appearance to sign books. You'll see that as you get a few of these under your belt, they get easier and easier, and you will become a pro at working them.

OTHER MARKETS

Once you've gotten your marketing plan together and have set everything in motion, it's tempting to sit back and wait to see what's going to happen. But don't stop there! Look into other markets – places that aren't readily apparent… is there another place that might be a possible market for your book?

Look For Relationships

Once you've placed your book in the obvious markets, look for other avenues that aren't so obvious. For example, if you have a barbeque cookbook that you've managed to get in bookstores, look beyond that. Think about places that sell barbeque grills – wouldn't your book fit perfectly on a shelf beside them? Or how about at a barbeque cook-off, at a table complete with food samples? The possibilities are endless, and you might even find a mail order catalog or website that specializes in barbeque products that would be excited about adding your book.

Those are the kinds of opportunities that you need to seek out – relationships between your book and other products that complement it.

Symbiotic Relationships

One such type of marketing relationship is known as "symbiotic." In a case like this, two different businesses establish a relationship that is mutually beneficial.

For example, a while back I was watching television and saw a commercial for a Las Vegas vacation package. It featured three days and two nights at one of the mega-resort/casinos on the Strip, and the deal looked very appealing. Included was a dinner at a legendary Vegas restaurant, and also a couple of tickets to one of the big-name evening shows. It struck me I was watching a perfect example of a symbiotic relationship in that vacation package – it was between the hotel, the restaurant and the show.

The resort makes their money from luring people into the casino, so when someone purchases the package and books a stay at the hotel it works to their advantage. The restaurant, of course, sells food. The evening show, on the other hand, makes money by selling tickets. The old days where food and shows were cheap in order to draw business to the hotel are long gone; today you can pay $100-$150 per seat to see arena shows such as Cirque du Soleil, Blue Man Crew, or Cher. If you were to break down the package, the hotel is contributing a discounted room, the restaurant is cutting the price of their meal, and the show is giving tickets at a discount price. When all this is put together, it is very attractive to a traveler – the business participants are attracting customers that might not otherwise stay at that hotel, eat at that restaurant, or attend that show... in fact, they might not even go to Las Vegas at all.

If a symbiotic relationship is going to succeed, it needs to have the following qualities:

- The businesses involved in the relationship are independent and most likely unique, but share some important aspect of the deal that serves their own needs.
- The symbiotic relationship has ongoing, continuous value. It will survive long-term, not just in the short run.
- The symbiosis is profitable for all parties, but no single partner will fail without it.

You're probably already thinking of possible relationships like this for your book. If you have a how-to greenhouse book, you might want to partner it with a nursery – the book is free with the purchase of $200 worth of plants, and the nursery pays you $12.00 for the book that you would normally charge $18.00 for, then you're getting sales (albeit at a discount) that you wouldn't have ordinarily have seen.

If symbiotic relationships provide a win/win for all parties, then you've achieved balance and mutual success.

Cross Selling

Cross selling is the concept of selling an additional product to an existing customer. The extra product sold should add value to the customer's experience.

One of the best examples of cross selling is done automatically by the mega-bookseller Amazon.com. You may notice that when you search for a book on any topic you are given a list of possible choices. When you click on one the web page presents you with the details on that book – and there's always a notation about halfway down the page that says, "People who bought this book also purchased this other one…" and they will display a related book, often at a discounted price if you buy the combo.

Another company uses another form of cross selling, even though the end result is not profit, but instead customer satisfaction. There is a very successful online movie rental company called Netflix.com – you'd have to be living in a cave if you haven't heard of them before. When you rent a movie, they make future recommendations based on that rental. For example, if you rent the John Wayne movie *Rio Bravo*, then they might recommend other westerns by the same actor such as *The Cowboys*, *Big Jake*, and *The Searchers*. The way that Netflix operates, however, is that you can rent as many movies per month as you can watch, at a single price. They don't see any extra revenue whether you rent twenty movies or just one. What they are getting out of this form of cross selling is increased customer satisfaction – after all, they're competing with giants such as Blockbuster, mom-and-pop video stores down the street from you, and also businesses using symbiotic services such as video stores within large groceries such as Albertson's, Kroger, etc.

While the concept of cross selling may be hard for the one-book author to implement, as you grow your product line it can fall naturally into place. For example, you can sell the book at one price, or the book and a related DVD presentation for a combined discount price. You'll see how products fit together into the model of cross selling as you increase your product line.

WRAPPING UP OUR MARKETING DISCUSSION

Did you notice that this section of the book that covers marketing is easily twice as long as any other section of the book?

Well, there's a reason for that – writing your book is just the beginning. Most successful authors spend, on order of magnitude, more time on marketing than they do writing and producing a book.

I hope that you are coming away from this section with a wealth of marketing knowledge, but more than that, I hope that you have learned to think like a marketing person. I want you to constantly be analyzing situations and opportunities, dissecting them as to how they can work to your advantage.

Section Five – And Finally…

PARTING REMARKS

I started seriously working on this book idea way back in 1996. Back then it was just a dream and a huge box full of scribbled notes and outlines and clippings. The world was a different place then.

With no internet and no real self publishing resources I was a 'babe in the woods' and my book writing and self publishing ideas were a part time activity. With a family to support and a busy life full of challenges, I had little time to spend on writing but I did keep at it, in snatches, in spare moments, on the odd weekend with nothing else to do, and over the years my boxes got bigger and heavier and the project began to take shape.

It seems like a long time doesn't it? I think if I had a book like this one when I started it would have been different.

There are two really important things I have to say at this point. First, much of the time spent with this book was wasted. What?! I struggled with this project for years because I didn't have a direction, a clear view of the big picture, an outline or writing system to help me keep on course, and proper tools to work with.

Secondly, I was trying to make this book perfect. It wasn't perfect then, it isn't now, nor will it ever be perfect! My point is that we need to know when to stop researching, exploring new ideas, rewriting page after page, and just get the darn thing finished. I find myself doing it again today...re-reading and tweaking... it's so tempting to jump back in and make a few changes... I've been doing it for a long time.

Now, you're going to get this book just the way it is. Yes, there are some new things on the internet that might be useful. Yes, I could work on the writing some more... a lot more. Yes, there are a few things I'd like to add, but I finally understood that I had an important message that might be helpful to some writers and it would be better to complete this book and get it into the marketplace where it might do some good.

A FEW PARTING REMARKS AND COMMENTS:

About Marketing, Social Marketing, and Networking

When I began working on the project there was no such thing as Social Marketing. I don't remember becoming aware of Facebook until maybe two years ago. I was probably the last one on earth to get a Google email account.

The Internet Marketing scene has unfolded before my very eyes as I worked on this book and made changes to it. In fact, the changes happened so frequently that I was never really able to keep up with them within these pages.

I did something better. I created a website for the book and have been writing and will always write about changes, new ideas and resources that prove to be useful to this body of authors.

The website addresses are below. One is for the hard copy books and the other is for eBooks. We keep them separate because of the completely different approach to the production and marketing and sales of the books. There are a lot of resources on both sites.

Please visit the sites and sign up for our newsletters to receive updates and pertinent news. Read the articles, make use of the resources, and please make comments at will, ask questions, and let us know if we can do anything to help you.

ABOUT EDUCATION

Don't let it hold you back…either way by having too much or way too little. It isn't the education that will get your book written and published… it's guts and determination and 'stick-with it' ability.

Some of the most important books of our time have been written by uneducated authors with something to say and a burning passion to say it.

If you want it bad enough you can get it done and even if the grammar and writing isn't top notch a good book on a hot topic with valuable information to share will always find its way into the hands of passionate readers.

Be with friends who will support you

Choose your friends wisely. Find supportive and loving friends who will encourage you, keep the 'Devil's Advocate' stuff to themselves, and know how to pamper your ego, protect your feelings, and help you along the way. A handful of supportive friends will be one of the most important tools in your bag.

WE ARE A FAMILY

I find myself drawn to writers like myself… those that aren't polished professionals, don't have a lot of experience or skills, but have the desire and the passion and work hard to get their book written and published.

I always feel the same way when we meet… like we are a family… I am pulled into their stories and histories and am fascinated by the experiences of this unique group of people.

Let's stay together, love and help each other, and as a group, with these beliefs and this remarkable support system, we have the power to individually and collectively change the world with our works.

I am committed to you and will always be available in any way possible, within my abilities, to work alongside of you as you forge ahead.

I BELIEVE IN YOU!

The rewards are there... financially or emotionally they are always there waiting for you.

Stand strong on your conviction, hold onto your belief in your topic and your work and your passions.

You can do it!

In the infamous words of Winston Churchill:

Never, never, never give up!

Resources:

Our publishing companies and websites:

www.hardcopypublishing.com

www.greenbarnbooks.com

Our marketing company:

www.webpmc.com

Our website design and hosting company:

www.blackduckwebdesign.com

www.ingramcontent.com/pod-product-compliance
Lightning Source LLC
Chambersburg PA
CBHW060300100426
42742CB00011B/1821